Praise for Tarot Grimoire

"Ethony is magical, so it's no wonder that she has created my favorite book blending tarot and magic. Filled to the brim with spells and exercises that will deepen both your witchcraft and tarot practices, you will find the *Tarot Grimoire* is both joyful and profoundly transformative, as all the best magic is! This is sure to be at the front of your tarot and magic bookshelf, as it is on mine."

—MADAME PAMITA, author of *Magical Tarot* and *The Book of Candle Magic*

"*Tarot Grimoire* is essential for anyone following a path of tarot, witchcraft, and magic. The way in which Ethony shares her spells, spreads, and her own magic in this book so openly, authentically, and generously makes it feel Ethony is right there with you. ... She is the real deal, a huge inspiration to the tarot and witchcraft community, and a beautiful person who cares so deeply about the work she does for others. This book is a true gift to her ever-growing community and to all those witches looking for a guide as knowledgeable and experienced as Ethony."

—VICTORIA "VIX" MAXWELL, author, soul reader, and Kundalini yoga teacher

T0243939

TAROT
GRIMOIRE

About the Author

Ethony Dawn has been reading the tarot for clients all over the world for more than twenty-five years. She is the creator of the Cosmic Wisdom Tarot, the Modern Love Tarot, and two other tarot decks. She has also created three oracle decks. Ethony is the headmistress of the Tarot Readers Academy, where she teaches the art of reading the tarot. Since 2016, she has been involved with an online coven, the Awakened Soul Coven, where she shares her decades of experience working with modern magic. Ethony lives in Vancouver, BC, with her family and three dogs.

TAROT
GRIMOIRE

ETHONY
DAWN

FOREWORD BY
**BENEBELL
WEN**

Spreads and Spells
for a Magical Life

Llewellyn Publications | Woodbury, Minnesota

FIRST EDITION
First Printing, 2024

Book design by R. Brasington
Cover art by AlbaBG
Cover design by Shannon McKuhen
Editing by Marjorie Otto
Card illustrations in the interior are from the *Tarot Original 1909 Deck* © 2021 with art created by Pamela Colman Smith and Arthur Edward Waite. Used with permission of Lo Scarabeo.
Interior card spreads and other illustratons by Llewellyn Art Department

Llewellyn Publications is a registered trademark of Llewellyn Worldwide Ltd.

Library of Congress Cataloging-in-Publication Data (Pending)
ISBN: 978-0-7387-7704-7

Llewellyn Worldwide Ltd. does not participate in, endorse, or have any authority or responsibility concerning private business transactions between our authors and the public.

All mail addressed to the author is forwarded, but the publisher cannot, unless specifically instructed by the author, give out an address or phone number.

Any internet references contained in this work are current at publication time, but the publisher cannot guarantee that a specific location will continue to be maintained. Please refer to the publisher's website for links to authors' websites and other sources.

Llewellyn Publications
A Division of Llewellyn Worldwide Ltd.
2143 Wooddale Drive
Woodbury, MN 55125-2989
www.llewellyn.com

Printed in the United States of America

Other Books by Ethony Dawn
Your Tarot Court (2019)

For my
magical bumblebees.

Contents

Foreword

Ethony and I became instant friends when we met in 2018 at the Tarot Readers Studio in New York. Prior to that I had served as faculty at her Tarot Readers Academy, joining in the inaugural year of her online tarot summer school, the first cartomancy program of its kind. A powerhouse thought and people leader, Ethony commands a talent for bringing together diverse ensembles, and you see this throughout all aspects of her work.

Her tarot philosophy is one of open arms, compassion, and inclusivity, integrating eclectic Paganism with whimsy and sass. *Take what resonates and leave the rest* has become her signature motto, one that has inspired students of tarot and witchcraft to embrace that same permissive, benevolent, and personally curated approach. Ethony fosters community while encouraging individual expression.

This is a book that unabashedly embraces the magic and mystery of tarot. It is a functional collection of spreads for readers of all capacities and a primer for a new generation of modern witchcraft. Covering the basics in divination, spellcasting, and ritual work, guided by seventy-eight tarot archetypes, *Tarot Grimoire* will be an essential reference in your magical library.

You will be guided on a self-empowering journey to revealing the mystic within, narrated by a voice of reason, of humour, and rich with the wisdom of your fairy godmother. Start with the tarot spread for the Magician to problem-solve, then boost your powers for tackling challenges with an empowerment tea spell. Receive the High Priestess's calling through her six-card spread, then craft psychic power anointing oil.

Explore the four elements through the minors. Cultivate self-mastery in the realm of the heart and emotions by way of the Cups. Reinvigorate yourself, your vitality, and explore pursuits of passion through the Wands. Come into full knowledge of your mind and fine-tune your communication skills with the Swords. Conclude the journey with appreciation for your body and surroundings by way of the Pentacles. Learn how to manifest prosperity, clear creative blocks, improve mental clarity, achieve both short-term and long-term goals, and embrace the many facets of love through seventy-eight beautiful, practical, and potent spells.

You'll work with river stones, charm bags, poppets, herb crafting, candle magic, crystals, essential oils, and so much more. These spells nudge you to see the magical potential in the everyday mundane. Before you throw out those oyster shells, pause to see how they might help you to harness the blessings of the Lovers. Master the metaphysical correspondences of spices in your kitchen pantry. Fully understand the power of the petition.

Ethony is a tarot spreads master, and I have enjoyed implementing many of her well-constructed spreads into my reading practice. To help confront and dispel bias so that I might see a situation with greater clarity and objectivity, I work with the Queen of Swords spread. The Tea of Peace recipe for the Ace of Cups is the perfect, delicious blend to sip on as I work with its accompanying Tap into Your Emotions five-card reading. Amplify your goal-setting with the Star card's Make It Happen spread, then on the next Full Moon, follow the affirming Make a Wish spell.

For months I kept pulling the Knight of Wands card, no matter which deck I used or the context of the reading—what tarot readers often call a "stalker card." So I consulted the *Tarot Grimoire* and looked up the Knight of Wands' associated spread. As the *Grimoire* offers, perhaps this stalker card is guiding me to actualize my soul's passion. With that stalker Knight of Wands as my significator card, I worked with the six-card spread, revealing what was missing from my life, what it was my soul wanted to explore at this time, and what first steps to take to embrace my soul's passion. Then I tried out the Winner Winner Spell. I can attest that the spell helped to achieve hard-won victories.

Death's Mediumship Spread, whether you believe in an afterlife or not, is a beautiful way to make sense of difficult endings, to experience closure through the spirit of what once was here with us in body. Work with Key XV: the Devil card to finally end self-destructive cycles. You're going to love the Tower card's Shock Absorption Talisman, a malachite macramé necklace to help you navigate the aftershock of sudden change. You'll love making the Ten of Swords incense time and time again to help you eradicate malignant energies in your vicinity.

In so many ways, Ethony reminds me of a twenty-first-century Etteilla. Her Tarot Readers Academy, spiritual business coaching through her Business Beehive, and her Awakened Soul Coven are not unlike Etteilla's New School of Magic. She is a deck creator like Etteilla, becoming an independent publisher of decks just as Etteilla had done. She has certified many an incredible professional tarot reader, teaching tarot to innumerable students like Etteilla, and exhibits the business savvy of Etteilla. She was one of the first to showcase pick-a-card collective readings on social media, spearheading that trend, and one of the first to take coven work global and online. Reflecting on her many achievements and contributions, Ethony has become a living fixture in the world of tarot, as Etteilla was in his time.

Tarot Grimoire is a compendium that will quickly expand your knowledge and experience in the Craft, all while deepening your relationship with the tarot. Card by card, spread by spread, spell after spell, acquiring recipes, learning rituals, and fostering personal growth, this handbook charts a tried and true path into the sacred dimension.

—Benebell Wen

Introduction

Welcome to *Tarot Grimoire*, a peek into my personal magical books and practice. This is a book that you can use in your daily life to read for yourself and others and to embody your readings for positive change well after the reading session is done.

The tarot has been a cornerstone of magical practice for centuries. Its adaptability and evolution have made it a go-to tool for diviners, coaches, teachers, and creatives, and that's just the tip of the tarot iceberg. I discovered tarot at the age of fifteen through my spiritual training in Wicca. Since then, I've been deeply connected to the tarot, and now, I'm passing on this wisdom to you. Over the years, I've explored various forms of divination, including oracle decks, runes, pendulums, charm casting, Lenormand, and more. Yet the tarot remains my steadfast companion. There's never a time when a deck is out of arm's reach.

Through building my relationship with the tarot and reading for thousands of people, I now have the honor of teaching the tarot. I've journeyed into each card and cast spells with all of the arcana. I've written books and helped others with this fantastic system.

I have notebooks full of custom tarot spreads that I've created for clients, my coven, and myself. I've got magical notebooks, grimoires, and Books of Shadows lining my shelf full of my favorite spells. So, it felt natural to combine all of this into one book. It's designed to be a comprehensive guide for tarot readers, witches, and magical practitioners eager to intertwine the realms of tarot and magic.

Throughout my magical journey, I've been lucky to have teachers and mentors share their knowledge with me and explain why an ingredient is used or give me a tip on the best item for what type of magic. I'm doing the same throughout *Tarot Grimoire*. The book has boxes with tips on tarot interpretation, art magic, herbs and spices, magical tools, and much more to give you some magical shortcuts and suggestions.

By working with the tarot spreads dedicated to each of the tarot cards and their companion tarot spell, you'll be living the magic of the tarot. You'll become the embodiment of the arcana, giving yourself the gift of living an intentional life. You'll embrace your inner strength and talents, build mindfulness and resilience, and learn about yourself and your place in the world.

Are you ready to dive in? Let's get the magic started!

Using The Tarot Grimoire

This book is meant to be used to bring the energetic vibration, lessons, and magic of the seventy-eight tarot cards to life. This is a book of practice. You can come to this book when you have a need and look up the corresponding tarot spread and spell or allow your tarot readings to lead you on your magical journey. Bend the spine, write in the pages, and highlight your favorite parts. The *Tarot Grimoire* can be used as a metaphysical blueprint for deepening your work with the tarot.

Here are some ways you can use this book, but remember that these are only suggestions. Your magic, your tarot, and your path are more important than someone else's way of doing things. Always remember that this is your journey. Take what resonates with you and leave the rest.

We all face difficult situations in life when something comes up that starts to disempower us. This is a great time to work with the spells and spreads in this book. Arming yourself with as much information and foresight as possible is never a bad idea. Knowledge is power, and when you give yourself the gift of careful consideration and reflection through a personalized tarot reading, you empower yourself to make the most out of the opportunity and avoid pitfalls. Let's face it: no one wants to hit unnecessary roadblocks that could've been avoided.

There will be seasons in your life when you pull the same tarot card over and over again in readings for yourself and others. Even when you think you've learned the lesson or you feel you know what the universe is trying to tell you, the card keeps showing up! When this happens, it's the perfect opportunity to sit with the many facets of the tarot card offered in its spread section to further understand why a specific card is making itself known. If the card still keeps showing up, it might be a hint that it's time to carry out its corresponding tarot spell. By moving your energy and focus from the intellectual knowledge of the cards to practice, you bring the knowledge down to earth. It becomes part of you and, therefore, easier to integrate its lessons in your life.

Magic is harnessing the natural flow, energies, and vibrations to bring lasting and influential change into your life. There are various techniques and skills a practitioner can use to achieve this. Many of these are presented in this book, and this is where you can find, through application, what works for you.

All magical users will agree that when you're ready and have a deep desire to create a life you genuinely love, magic is an excellent tool to aid in your evolution. Working with the spells within this book will ensure that you're keeping your vibration where you want it to be. They will help you to stop worrying about the future possibilities of co-creating your future with the universe and focus on the here and now.

By using the tarot spreads in this book, you'll be able to look at every angle of your journey and personal growth, ensuring that it will generate lasting and powerful change. You can also look up any of the tarot spreads when you are carrying out a tarot reading for someone else to help them on their path.

There are many spells and tarot spreads that focus on healing, and for good reason. When you want to heal from something and move on from the past, having supportive tools for your recovery and revival are incredibly empowering. Healing is an ongoing journey. Once you've decided you're ready to take it on, you'll find your tarot deck can be a priceless tool to guide you. The spreads and spells presented within can be used as a supplement to all of your healing, whether it's spiritual, physical, mental or emotional. While this book, the tarot spreads, and the spells within it can be powerful agents of transformation, this is not a complete healing system. Please acknowledge your limits and always seek medical treatment when needed. We all require help at times, and we don't know what we don't know. Holistic healing requires you to look at healing your mind, body, energy, and soul.

If you're a student of the tarot, the spreads and spells within can be used throughout your studies as a way to comprehend the different aspects of the individual cards. You can do this by working through the deck, starting at the Fool and ending at the King of Pentacles. Or you can use it as a supplement for your card-a-day draws.

You don't have to use the spells in this book to access the magic and meaning of the tarot cards. Not every tarot reader will be into casting spells. There is no one right way to work with the tarot. That's the beauty of the tool. Know, however, that they'll be there if you ever want to try your hand at some magic. You may be surprised at just how easy and effective it is.

The spells in this book are easy to use. Magic doesn't need to be complicated in order to work. Most importantly, you are ready to do the work energetically, magically and in your everyday life. The ingredients and items required for the magic are as accessible as possible. Effective spells shouldn't have you breaking your bank account or maxing out your credit card to access them.

Everything in this book is meant to be used and can be personalized and adapted to your practice and needs. Every tarot reader and magical practitioner has their own brand of magic and method of reading. You bring your energy and wisdom to each tarot reading and spellcasting. Magical books, such as *Tarot Grimoire*, should be a representation of the practitioner's working practice that evolves as they do. I've often found spells that I like the foundations of and then rewrote them in my Book of Shadows with any personalizations or substitutions on ingredients I needed to make. I encourage you to do this with the spells, and even the tarot spreads in this book.

Using the Tarot Spreads in this Book

Tarot spreads are an excellent container and road map for tarot readings. They're fantastic for allowing you to apply context to the cards, as the positions in the spreads will tell you where to focus. Each tarot card has a different message depending on the context of the reading and the position of the layout. Using a tarot spread takes out some of the guesswork.

If you read the tarot alongside your intuition, trust what your inner knowing is telling you. Tarot spreads also give you a place to start and end the reading. When you begin your journey with the tarot, this is truly helpful. You won't have to worry about having the "right" number of tarot cards in your spread or knowing if you've covered everything you need to in your reading.

When you work with the tarot spreads in the *Tarot Grimoire*, you don't need to remove the tarot card for which the spread is created. You want to use your complete deck when reading with the spreads. You should watch out for the corresponding card if it shows up in your reading. For example, if you're using the Take the Leap tarot spread that corresponds with the Fool and the Fool card comes up in that reading, then the card holds extra weight in that reading.

The tarot spreads are designed to be used with a tarot deck, but you can use oracle cards with these spreads if you wish. You can also use any other cartomancy system, like playing cards, runes, or charms. Have fun playing with divination and the different tools and methods out there. Allow your intuition to take the lead and lean into everything with a curious mind. If you feel drawn to working with an oracle deck, then use one.

Use the tarot spreads presented within whenever you want. You can use them when reading the cards for yourself, others and even clients if you're a professional tarot reader. There are no hard and fast rules with these tarot spreads. You can make the rules! If you've never picked up a tarot deck and you've felt drawn to this book, this may be the invitation you've been waiting for.

Your Own Magical Grimoires

This book may be the first step you're taking on your magical journey, or it could be added to your library. Either way, building your own magical records is integral to your spiritual development.

You can have one book with all of your magical work, tarot readings, dreams, and journal entries in it, or you can have separate books for each. When you give yourself a place to store all of your magical experiences, you'll see that your experiences are the best teachers. You can review where you've had success and what you may have missed or want to improve upon.

Recording your tarot readings will help you gain confidence in your ability to read the cards. It'll aid you in building your own book of meanings and deepen your understanding of the tarot cards in real life. You can also go back and check to see if any reading predictions come to pass.

There are so many beautiful journals and books on the market that you can purchase and handwrite your spells, readings, and experiences in. Or you can create your own. If you're not into handwriting or don't have the time, there are wonderful apps you can use to record everything. I even have a complete Book of Shadows on my Google Drive! The important thing is that it works for you.

Working Safely with Magical Herbs and Spices

The use of magical herbs and spices, as described within, should be approached with caution and respect. While many of the herbs and spices mentioned have been used historically for various purposes, including spiritual and medicinal, it is essential to remember that not all herbs and spices are safe for consumption or topical application. Some may be toxic, cause allergic reactions, or interact negatively with medications or other herbs. Always consult with a qualified healthcare professional before using any new herb or spice, especially for medicinal purposes. The use of certain herbs and spices may have deep cultural, religious, or spiritual significance in various traditions. Approach their use with respect and awareness of their origins and meanings. Always source herbs and spices from reputable suppliers. Be aware of issues like overharvesting, which can endanger certain plant species and harm ecosystems. Store herbs and spices in a cool, dry place away from direct sunlight. This will help maintain their potency and reduce the risk of spoilage.

By continuing to read and apply the information in this book, you acknowledge that you are doing so at your own risk. The author and publisher disclaim any liabilities or losses, direct or indirect, that might arise from using or misusing the information contained herein.

Chapter 1
Magic and Casting Spells

Humans have been casting spells for hundreds of thousands of years. Evidence of this has been collected throughout history through cave paintings, tools, temples, relics, stories, and myths. Humanity and the realm of magic have always been looking for a way to connect with each other. It may be because we come from a source, magic, cosmic energy, or primordial ooze—whatever you want to call it. When we come into the world in this human form, separated from that magic, we seek it out, consciously or unconsciously. The truth is, we're never truly cut off from that energy. It's just that these dense meat sac bodies, the environment we were raised in, and the modern world can make it harder to access.

There are magical practices all over the world, spells that have been handed down through families, magical traditions, and reconstructed practices. Contrary to popular belief, magic is not about breaking the laws of nature. It's about learning how to work with these natural laws to bring about desired changes in your life. Magic allows you to harness your inner power and that of the natural world and bring those two into alignment.

One of the most effective and powerful ways to focus and direct these energies is with the archetypes of the tarot. The energies, symbols, and meanings within the tarot cards are the perfect partner to manifest your inventions through magic. When you use the tarot in your spellwork, you're giving yourself access to the collective energy of the tarot cards' archetypes.

Anyone from any background can be a magic user. You don't need to be a witch, Wiccan, wizard, Pagan, or devotee of the Flying Spaghetti Monster in the sky to practice powerful and impactful magic. Anyone who says this wants to be a gatekeeper of someplace within them that needs healing. Most people cast spells without even realizing they're doing so. Wishing on a star, tossing a coin in a well or fountain, and even blowing out candles on a birthday cake are all magic spells. You're carrying out a magical act whenever you write something down.

Spells are like recipes. Sometimes, you won't have an ingredient that's listed. When this happens, don't fret. You can make alterations to the spell to make it work. Not all herbs and spices or ingredients are going to be accessible in your geographic location. Others listed in the spells may already be in your kitchen or easy to find. The most important thing to remember is that your intention, work, and follow-through are just as important as the spell itself.

When it comes to magic and casting successful spells, you need to be willing to meet the magic halfway. Casting a spell and using magic are one part of a successful partnership when it comes to manifesting change. You cannot expect to cast a spell for a new job and do nothing in your everyday life to help make it happen. You need to write your resume, reach out to your networks, practice your interviewing skills, and apply for jobs. Check in with your tarot cards and do a reading on the potential jobs you're applying for. Ask the tarot if there is anything else you can do to make your success imminent. Pull a card and put the wisdom that the card has to offer into practice.

Magic isn't energetic DoorDash; what you do in the world matters. If you're able to consistently make small changes in your daily life that move you toward the goal of your spell, you're making its success exponentially more likely. Casting a spell sends your intentions and energy out into the universe. It opens the door, allowing the desired outcome to come back in. Doing something in the real world shows the magic you're serious.

You'll find when you've created successful magic, it has a wonderful way of presenting you with opportunities you would not have thought possible. Try not to get too attached to the outcome or have the spell work precisely as you expected. The universe is so much better than you are at miracles and manifestation. Let it bring big magic to your life. Let the magic breathe and grow as you do. Don't limit yourself or your magic.

Every spellcaster has made mistakes when it comes to casting spells. I've added the wrong ingredient in a spell. I've cast the spell on a day of the week that wasn't aligned with the outcome as much as another day was. I also nearly burnt down a magic shop because I burnt a magical petition in a bronze cauldron that got so hot it melted the feet off and tipped the burning contents all over the floor. Thankfully, no one was hurt, and the store still stands. A vital lesson was learnt that day. Use a cast iron cauldron for burning magical petitions!

Just know it's okay to make mistakes and find your way of being a magical practitioner. Try new magical techniques. Don't be afraid if you accidentally mispronounce the name of a plant spirit or deity. Joy and magic go together like peas and carrots. Not only will you have more fun in life if you don't take everything so seriously, but joy is a high vibration, and magic loves that energy. There are people who carry out their entire magical practice in an earnest way. Everything is calculated precisely and formally, and that's cool if that is the way you want to work your magic. Even the most meticulous magical practitioners will occasionally make mistakes. Don't be too hard on yourself when you do.

If you lose or damage a tarot card when working with a magical spell, know that it's done its work. That's a positive sign that your magic is potent and going to yield good results. You can retire the card by putting it in your Book of Shadows next to the notes of your spellcasting. You can replace the card that's been lost or damaged in many ways. Reach out to the publisher or creator of the deck, and they'll likely send you a replacement card.

Weaving the tarot and magic together can give you the ability to deepen your spiritual knowledge and transform your life. Allow it to be a fun collaboration; the seventy-eight cards are your magical cheerleaders, showing you just how accessible magic is.

Spells vs. Rituals

While you'll find that the terms *spells* and *rituals* are used interchangeably in many texts, they do have distinct characteristics and purposes for the person carrying them out. The magical applications in the *Tarot Grimoire* are spells. However, knowing the differences between spells and rituals for your journey is essential.

Spells are a way to harness and manipulate natural energies through the use of specific tools, actions, and energy work. They're acts carried out to bring about particular outcomes. Spells are a form of intentional energy work where you direct your will, symbolic tools, and actions to manifest a desired result. Spells can be simple charms to get a good parking spot in a crowded mall or more involved, like a seven-day candle spell that builds in power daily.

A ritual is any action that's done with a defined intention. Often symbolic in nature, they are performed in a specific order and manner. Most rituals have a number of steps that the practitioner carries out that may be repeated or done at a particular time. These times are often connected with holidays, rights of passage, and religious and spiritual ceremonies. Many rituals are performed to commune with the Divine or connect with specific ancestors or guides. Rituals can be performed as an individual or with other people. The most important thing about ritual is that it has profound meaning for the one conducting it. The intention of the ritual is focused on the act itself and the spiritual connection it nurtures for the practitioner.

Both spells and rituals will often use tools, symbols, mantras, chants, music, and ingredients in their work. Rituals and spells are both ways to create sacred space and enrich your life. Many rituals will have an element of spellcasting in their work. For example, if you're a practicing modern witch who's performing a Full Moon ritual, there may be elements in the ritual where communion is done by calling in the four natural elements and a deity the witch wants to work with. Then, there may be a part of the ritual where spell work is done through petitioning the deity to aid them in manifesting the change they desire, for example, by making a healing pillow for themselves. After that magical work is complete, the ritual concludes with the actions of thanking the Divine and magical elements and closing their magic circle. This is just one example of how rituals and spells can be present in the same overall work.

The critical difference between a ritual and a spell is in the intention behind them. Spells are goal-oriented, whereas rituals are connection-oriented.

Cosmic Energies and Spells

Astronomy and astrology are fields of specialization that can take a lifetime to master. There is so much to learn about the planets, the zodiac signs, and the influence these have on our lives. Before you cast your first tarot spell, let's look at some of the primary cosmic energies that will help your spells be impactful in your life. Of course, life will drop challenges and opportunities at different times, whether the cosmic timing is aligned to tackle it or not, so don't become too obsessed with getting your cosmic timing right for magic. Your energy and intentions are going to be the driving force of your life and magic. Let's look at one of the biggest influences in magical practice: the Moon.

Why Are We Obsessed with the Moon?

Myth and legend have been attached to the Moon since our ancestors told stories to each other around a fire, under an open sky. Goddesses and gods all over the world are associated with the Moon and their relationship to the universe and other heavenly bodies. Our bodies are drawn to the Moon just as the oceans' tides are influenced by her pull. It's no wonder that magical workers and mystics love the Moon. The Moon's illumination is ever-changing. Under that shifting mysterious light, the Moon witnesses everything done at night. The phases of the Moon mark the cycles of her light in the sky and the power she wields over our magic. The spells in this book will often ask you to cast them under a specific phase, with the focus being the five major phases. A Moon phase guide or an app on your phone will help you track the phases of the Moon in your location.

The New Moon

When there is a tiny sliver in the sky of the Moon's light, you will know it is a New Moon. The New Moon is a magical time of growth, new opportunities, beginnings, and manifesting goals. It's a perfect time to perform spells that are required to increase in strength and intensity. Examples of this type of magic are spells to find new employment or new relationships.

The Waxing Moon

This is when the magic and light of the Moon increase every night. This occurs after the New Moon all the way to the Full Moon. Any spell that requires constant growth and building strength is ideal for casting as the Moon waxes. It's a time of increasing power, and it's an excellent time to cast spells that require time to fulfill their potential. Examples of this type of magic are spells for manifesting more significant amounts of money or maintaining motivation for large projects.

The Full Moon

This is when the Moon's light is brightest, and the magical energy she lends has reached its peak. Any spell can be cast at this time. Casting spells the day before, the day of, and the day after are the most potent for magic. Any psychic or divination work will also be powerful during the Full Moon. If you have an issue or goal that you need a cosmic power punch to manifest or change, this is the time to cast your spell.

The Waning Moon

The Waning Moon is the phase where the light and power of the Moon are dimming night after night. It happens after the Full Moon until the Dark Moon. At this time, the Moon is drawing in its power and releasing its hold of influence. Cast spells with themes of release, banishment, or withdrawal. Examples of these spells include removing an obstacle in your life, banishing a bad habit, or letting go of an old relationship.

The Dark Moon

The Dark Moon is the time of the Moon's phase when there is no moonlight in the sky. Some traditions say it's not a time to cast any spells but a time to reflect, meditate, and prepare for the next New Moon. If you want to cast magic at this time, spells with significant transitions in life, binding, and endings are recommended. Examples of spells you may cast at this time are mediumship spells, letting go of a long-term commitment, and a failed project.

Throughout the years of my magical practice and mentoring people in my coven, I've always recommended that each person form their own relationship with the Moon and her phases. Some magical people love working with Full Moon energy; others find it exhausting and draining. Chart how you feel during the waxing and waning of the Moon. Trust your intuition and create your own Moon magic.

Colors and Magic

Colors play an essential part in magic. When you use a specific color, you add its vibrational and magical properties to your work. The applications of color in magic are wide. You can use the vibration of color when you choose items in your magic. Candles, crystals, altar cloths, paints, flowers, and all other spell ingredients in the corresponding color add energy to your work.

Each color has its own associated keywords and applications in magic. Use the chart below to see what color is best to use in each type of magic.

White	Energy, new beginnings, substitute for any color
Red	Passion, energy, change, courage, creativity
Orange	Health, balance, happiness, harvest, courage
Yellow	Communication, learning, travel, joy, happiness, vitality
Green	Love, healing, prosperity of all kinds, growth, money, prosperity
Blue	Peace, justice, career, emotional issues
Violet/Purple	Psychic development, spirit, royalty
Pink	Love, romance, family, heart matters, friends
Brown	Stability, possessions, grounding
Silver	The Goddess, mysteries, the Moon, prophecy
Gold	The God, prosperity, success
Black	Protection, endings, boundaries, power

Magical Tools and Correspondences

I love nothing more than going to local magical stores and browsing the crystals, books, and tools. If you have the opportunity to get your magical items from a local store, it's always wonderful to support local businesses. The tools recommended for your tarot spells are meant to be used, so consider practicality over aesthetics when adding anything to your collection.

Following is a list of essential tools to get you started. You don't need to go and purchase or collect everything all at once. Finding unique pieces slowly as you learn new magical techniques is fun. No magical tool should see you breaking the bank.

You can also use a lot of items in your kitchen as magical tools. Why make things more complicated than they need to be? A lot of what you have around your home will be perfect for casting spells. However, having a separate area to store your tools away from your everyday utensils is a good idea. You don't want to accidentally eat candle wax because you used a kitchen knife to carve your spell candle and then put it back in your drawer.

Many magical practitioners will make their own tools. One of the advantages of making your tools is that your energy is going to be infused into the tool. It will be a very effective extension of yourself.

Clear quartz: Clear quartz is a very versatile crystal, and an excellent clear quartz point can be used in your magical work often. Clear quartz is perfect for meditation, directing energy, and connecting with spirit guides. It's also a fantastic crystal to amplify the power of your tarot readings. This is the stone that will be used as a substitute for other crystals in your spells and practice. When selecting crystals for your tarot spells, purchase smaller stones that are only a couple of dollars. It's good to have a mix of pointed and tumbled stones.

Flame-resistant container: Cauldrons are iconic symbols of witchcraft, not just because of Shakespeare or the commercialization of Halloween. They're solid and adaptable; you can create so much magic with them. They can hold water, burn items, and serve as vessels for creating spell blends, charging moonwater, and being used as scrying devices. You can get a fancy cauldron from a New Age store, but you can also find them at reasonable prices at army supply and outdoor stores. Never mix your magical cauldron with everyday cooking pots. If you use a cauldron for magic, keep it for magic use only.

Candle snuffer: Candle snuffers have both practical and magical applications, which is why you need one. They prevent candle wax from splattering all over your workspace and tarot cards and ensure the magic isn't blown away when extinguishing your candles.

Moon tracker: Tracking the Moon's phases and signs is fundamental in spellcasting. Numerous journals, apps, and calendars can assist you in keeping track of lunar movements. It doesn't matter what you use as long as you can reference it easily when doing your magical planning or reading the tarot.

Candles: Candle magic is adaptable and straightforward. The ways you can use candles in your practice are vast. Slowly gathering candles of all shapes and colors for your apothecary is a good idea. The best colors to start with are white and black. Wish candles are ideal due to their size and affordability. You can even use birthday candles in a pinch.

Herbs and spices: There are magic herbs in your kitchen right now that you can use for your spells. Look at starting your magical herbs and spices collection with basil, cinnamon, bay leaves, rosemary, thyme and oregano. If you're able to find or even dry your own rose petals and lavender flowers, these are often used in spells. Salt is vital in magic. It's a protective substance and should always be in stock in your apothecary.

Colored ribbon: Multiple tarot spells in this book use ribbons of different colors. Dollar stores are a great place to source these. Don't forget to save ribbons from any gifts you may receive, as they can be reused for spells.

Pen and paper: Writing is a spell, so there's no surprise that you'll be using paper and pens of different colors in many of these tarot spells. You don't need fancy paper made by hereditary witches under a Full Moon with dragon's blood ink for magic. Any pen and paper will do.

Remember, while these tools are essential, your intention is the most crucial ingredient in any spell or magical work. You don't need expensive or specialized tools for a satisfying and effective witchcraft practice. Your focus and commitment are what truly matter.

Magical Workspaces and Altars

Many witches and magical practitioners have a dedicated space in their homes where they can work their magic and have room for devotional items. There are many different uses for altars. Devotional altars are often used for work with the Sacred Divine, gods, and goddesses. Ancestral altars are often created for daily ancestor work. Magical altars are a dedicated workspace for spells, magic preparations such as tool making and even tarot and oracle readings. I personally have more than one altar in my space. I have a devotional altar with statues of the deities I work with and a working stone circle. I also have an extensive working altar.

Not everyone is "out of the magical broom closet." Some people live at home or in an environment where they will be judged for their beliefs and practices. You may live with someone who won't respect your tools and may disturb your magical workings. Some people also don't like sharing their magic with others and would rather keep their work private.

If you don't have the room or opportunity to have a dedicated magical workspace or altar, here are a couple of suggestions to work around it. A larger wooden jewelry box, a small suitcase, or even a sturdy shoe box can be turned into a portable altar and magic space that can be put away after use. You can even get a small padlock if you want to lock it for safekeeping. Use a large tea tray as an altar. I love tea trays as they're usually wooden and can be moved with ease. Do all your magical spell work in the kitchen, and then make sure you put everything away when you've finished.

Energetic Hygiene

Maintaining your energetic hygiene is as crucial as taking care of your physical health, especially for tarot readers and people who perform any energy work. Just as we pick up physical dirt and grime as we carry out our daily activities, we also gather energetic detritus. This can come from the people we interact with, our environments, and even our emotions and thoughts. If this isn't cleared out regularly, it can lead to feelings of heaviness, tiredness, confusion, and a whole lot more unpleasant sensations. It will also make your tarot readings muddy, and your connection to your intuition will dull.

Regular energetic hygiene practices will ensure that you restore balance to your energy fields. You'll also be able to maintain a more positive vibration, and your intuition will be more precise. Some of the best ways to keep your energetic hygiene sparkly are as simple as swimming in a natural body of water. The ocean's salt is an added bonus as salt is protective in nature and an excellent cleanser. A good salt body scrub will do wonders if you don't have access to a swimmable lake, river, or ocean. If you can hang eucalyptus leaves in your shower, you're bringing the protective and cleansing magic of the plant into your daily shower.

Having a go at grounding and centering techniques is essential. Working with the tarot and magic will see you activating your higher chakras and energies. It's important to balance that out regularly. Grounding involves connecting with the energy of Gaia, Mother Earth, to stabilize and balance your energy. You can ground yourself by spending time in nature, visualizing roots extending from your feet into the Earth, or using grounding crystals like hematite or smoky quartz.

Shielding practices are valuable in maintaining your space and energy. When you shield, you protect your energy from external influences. There are multiple ways you can effectively shield yourself. You can create an energetic shield through visualization. This is also an excellent way to stretch your psychic muscles and work on developing your clairvoyance. You can also shield by using affirmations or wearing protective crystals like black tourmaline or amethyst.

Having a meditation practice and being mindful of your inner dialogue will aid your energy in staying balanced. Your meditations may only be a five-minute session before you go to bed or even in your car before work. These practices help you stay present and aware of your energy and allow you to notice any shifts or imbalances in your energy and address them promptly.

Energy healing practices are going to aid you in keeping your emotional bodies clear. Working with Reiki, sound healing, yoga, qigong, cord cutting, and chakra balancing can help clear blockages and restore the flow of energy in your body. Putting on your favorite song and having a dance party is also a way to shake off any stifling energies around you. These are just some of the energy practices you can learn throughout your practice. Reiki work is also an excellent way to bring energy healing into your tarot readings.

Never underestimate the power of having healthy boundaries. When you learn to embrace your boundaries, you're intentionally letting people and the universe know what you will and will not accept in your life. It will also allow you to distance yourself from energy-draining situations or relationships. Maintaining your boundaries is a crucial part of maintaining your energetic hygiene.

Cleansing your environment and your tarot decks is essential to keeping your channels open and clear and your living space pleasant. When you read with your tarot deck often, you may occasionally find that your tarot deck is giving you muddy readings or may even feel a little energetically sticky. When you cleanse your space or tarot deck, you're clearing away negative or stagnant energies.

You can cleanse your personal energy and living spaces through practices like smoke cleansing. Open all of your windows and allow air to flow through your area. Take a salt bath, or use sound healing with bells, drums, singing bowls, or tuning forks.

Cleansing your tarot deck with positive energy is not a requirement to be a good tarot reader and get accurate readings. However, the more you're able to sense and work with the subtle energies of the universe, the more you may want to embrace some of these recommendations.

You can store your tarot deck with a piece of black tourmaline or smoky quartz gemstones. Both of these crystals will clear any lower vibration energies from the deck. Put your tarot deck back in order and place it under the light of the Full Moon to cleanse and charge your deck. A windowsill is the perfect place for this. Even if the Moon can't be seen on a cloudy night, the Moon's light will still work. The Moon is deeply connected to intuition, so this is a fantastic practice to do regularly. You can also smoke cleanse your deck with your favorite cleansing herbs, resins, and woods.

Your energy is precious. Taking care of your energetic hygiene is an act of self-love and self-care that supports your overall well-being and spiritual growth.

The Morals of Spellcraft

Each magical worker is going to have their own belief system when it comes to the morals of casting spells. Some people believe in a "golden rule" or have their own moral code that they follow. Depending on your cultural practices and background, different magical workings may be entirely normal for you to practice but off-limits for others. These are challenges you're going to face with your magical work. Reflect on how you feel about the morals of spellcasting.

One common rule a lot of magical practitioners follow is not to focus your magic on a specific person. Trying to change someone's free will is a big no-no. If you wouldn't want someone to do that to you, don't do it to others.

If you're carrying out a healing or protective spell for your own child, this is just an extension of the natural healing and protection you have toward them as a parent or guardian. I would get permission from the parent of a child that isn't mine, even if it's for a close friend or family member.

When it comes to casting spells for work or money, there is more than enough for everyone. More than one applicant will be going for a position for most jobs. You have every right to work your magic for a promotion you've been working toward. There is more than one job available in the world, so you're not shutting down everyone else's ability to find work.

Understanding the circumstances of any work you do is also essential. Are you willing to live with them after? Ultimately, you have to find where your magical ethics lie. It's a decision only you can make.

Hexing, Cursing, Banishing, Oh My!

Every magical practitioner will have their own perspective on spells and rituals intended to harm or be less than pleasant. People's backgrounds, cultures, beliefs, and personal ethics are going to play a part in what kind of magic they work with. You have to be okay with yourself at the end of the day and with the consequences of your actions. If you see nothing wrong with hexing a person who has wronged you, that's your prerogative.

Be the change you want to see in the world. No one is perfect; however, many people on spiritual paths work consciously to align with their core beliefs and values. If you enjoy being in inclusive spaces, you're more likely to create those throughout your life. You attract what you send out into the world. Trying to be the best person you can be doesn't mean you won't step over your moral lines sometimes or make mistakes. You're only human. The good news is that you always have the opportunity to try again, choose a different option, and create positive outcomes in your life rather than adding more negativity into the world.

There is a theory that you have to be able to hex someone to heal them, as they are different sides of the same coin. Some practitioners will work to understand negative magical work to help heal others. Many healers don't ever touch anything remotely harmful.

Don't jump to conclusions if you think you've been hexed or had some negative magic sent your way. Belief is a powerful thing. If you believe someone has power over you, you make it more likely for them to do so. One of my all-time favorite movies *Labyrinth* has a solid affirmation for power recall from the main character, Sarah: "You have no power over me."

The energy in your home may just be stale. You may find as much benefit from a good spring clean or carrying out one of the energy hygiene practices suggested earlier in this chapter.

It's advisable not to have mirrors in your bedroom, especially if they face your bed. The same goes for televisions. Both are often believed to act as spirit portals. There's a notion that mirrors, especially during sleep, can jolt your spirit back into your body, potentially disrupting your rest. If you have these items in your bedroom, consider covering them with a shawl or removing them entirely.

Be wary of individuals who demand exorbitant amounts of money to remove curses or hexes. Such demands can be indicative of predatory behavior. While some argue that paying for magical services is valid, it's essential to be cautious about the price tag, especially if it's someone messaging you out of the blue or if the practitioner continually demands more money. Additionally, never hand over personal jewelry to such individuals, as there's a high likelihood you might never get it back.

It's crucial to approach magic with respect and understanding. Avoid dabbling in energies, magical modes, and unfamiliar entities. If you come across an incantation or a symbol that you don't understand, it's wise to either research it thoroughly or refrain from using it. Think of it this way: You wouldn't invite an unknown person into your home, so why would you invoke a deity or entity you know nothing about into your sacred space?

Last, prioritize your health. While it might sound cliché, the well-being of your physical body directly impacts your energetic body and its protective barriers. This includes staying hydrated, ensuring you get enough sleep, and taking care of your mental health. Every aspect of your health plays a role in your overall well-being. On days when maintaining optimal health feels challenging, remember to be kind to yourself. After all, we're all human, and it's essential not to overlook the significance of our health in our magical practices.

Before You Cast

Being well-informed and prepared is crucial before you carve your first spell candle. The following guidelines will ensure that your magical practices are both practical and safe.

First and foremost, when a spell requires the use of essential oils, herbs, resins, or spices, it's imperative to do your due diligence. Just because an ingredient is listed in a spellbook doesn't mean it's universally safe. Many herbs can interact negatively with certain medications; some are outright toxic. Essential oils, while potent, can be harmful to young children and pets or might even trigger allergic reactions in some individuals. Always conduct thorough research to ensure that any ingredient you use is safe for your specific circumstances.

As you prepare to cast a spell, it's beneficial to consider the practical steps you'll take in your daily life to complement the magic. Before initiating the spell, draft a list of mundane actions that will align with your magical intentions. Ask yourself: What proactive steps should I take? Are there habits I need to abandon? Taking immediate action post-spell empowers you and keeps your energy tuned to the spell's purpose.

When a spell involves ingesting herbs or spices or perhaps using them in teas, always source these ingredients from trustworthy suppliers. While growing and harvesting your own is ideal, opt for organic herbs if that's not feasible. They often offer the best quality. However, remember that magic is adaptable. Adjust the spell to fit your practice if certain ingredients are unavailable or beyond your budget.

Magic should never be used as an excuse to evade responsibility. True magic demands accountability. If you're seeking the fruits of your magical labor, you must also be prepared to own the process that leads to those results. Your ethical compass is personal, but at the very least, be responsible for your actions. Magic isn't a substitute for real-world effort or a shield from consequences.

Last, always read through the entire spell multiple times before beginning. Familiarizing yourself with each step ensures you won't overlook any details. This is especially vital if you wish to tailor the spell to your personal needs or circumstances.

Tarot Interpretation Tip

When looking for a tarot card to point to a yes, no, or a maybe, some cards will be easily aligned to an answer. For example, the Three of Swords is a clear no, and the Sun is a clear yes. A valuable tarot exercise is to write a list of the seventy-eight tarot cards and put your yes or no answers next to it so you can refer to it anytime. If you struggle with allocating a response, go with your initial intuitive feeling.

Before You Wave
Your Wand Around Spread

A technique that I was taught when I started my training in Wicca and Modern Witchcraft was to consult a form of divination before casting any spell. Sometimes, the divine timing isn't suitable for your working because there is more at play than you realize. Maybe you've forgotten to consider something or there is a more direct non-magic way to get the job done. This tarot spread has been a constant companion in my Book of Shadows and one that I work with before I do any significant magical work.

It's unnecessary to do this tarot spread before you cast all spells, if you're working on a quick magic spell or casting something that you know already feels right. This spread is a mystical quality assurance check to avoid the spell failing or not working as desired. You always have the choice of what to do, no matter what a tarot spread may say.

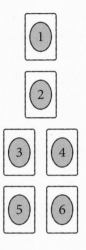

1. Is casting this spell a good idea/in alignment with my highest good?
2. What else do I need to consider before I cast this spell?
3. What mundane action do I need to take before I cast the spell?
4. What mundane action do I need to take after I cast the spell?
5. What will happen if I cast the spell?
6. What will happen if I don't cast the spell?

Chapter 2
Reading the Tarot Cards

Not all card decks are the same. There are oracle decks, Lenormand decks, playing card decks, kipper decks, and tarot decks. They can all be used for divination purposes and also for self-reflection and personal work. It doesn't mean that one is better than the other.

This book is a tarot grimoire, so working with a tarot deck is recommended. You can use other forms of card decks for the spreads and use the spells at any time, but the content is aligned with the tarot.

Some decks on the market call themselves tarot decks but aren't actually tarot decks at all. If you're new to the tarot, here are some of the identifying factors of a tarot deck. Tarot card decks have seventy-eight cards. They have twenty-two major arcana cards and fifty-six minor arcana cards. The deck has four suits. Commonly, they are the Cups, the Wands, the Pentacles, and the Swords. The minor arcana has a tarot court with sixteen cards. These are the Pages, Knights, Queens, and Kings. Many modern decks change the names of these court cards, but they remain in the deck.

Some tarot decks will have additional bonus cards. You can keep these in your deck or remove them. It's entirely up to you.

Picking the Perfect Tarot Deck

Selecting a tarot deck should be a personal experience. Artistic styles, colors, symbols, and interpretations will speak to you in unique ways through the tarot. Always work with the tarot deck that you feel most drawn to. If you're going to be working with the deck often, you want to enjoy the images and themes of your magical tool. Some tarot readers like to have different decks for the seasons of the year or for special occasions. You can swap out your tarot decks with the seasons or special events or work with the same deck all year round. As your tarot deck collection grows, you'll find that you may like to work with different tarot decks for themed tarot readings and magical workings.

The artwork and theme of your tarot decks will lend themselves to different magical work and readings. There are tarot decks that are explicitly created for love tarot readings that will work well for love spells. Animal-themed tarot decks will be perfect for working with your pets, and modern tarot decks are great for career advancement work.

You can use any tarot deck system with *Tarot Grimoire*. The best tarot deck is one that you love working with. I read and reference a lot of Rider-Waite-Smith-style decks. This was the first tarot system that I was introduced to when I was learning tarot. I fell in love with the system, and I've stuck with it as my primary tarot system ever since. There are a number of references and resources on this system and decks with different themes and styles. You can find a tarot deck no matter what you are drawn to.

Storing Your Tarot Deck

There are many options for storing your tarot decks. Tarot cards are a tool, and it's best to have the tools that you'll use often close at hand. You can keep your tarot decks in the boxes they came in or make or buy special boxes and bags for your decks.

Silk and velvet are popular materials used to store tarot cards. Wrapping your deck in a cloth made of these materials not only provides physical protection, it is also believed to shield the deck from negative energies. When you wrap your cards, you're enveloping them in a cocoon of safety, ensuring that they remain clean and energetically insulated. Place a piece of selenite crystal in your wrap with your cards for extra protection.

Wooden boxes are widely available and customizable. They're a sturdy and natural way to store your tarot cards. Wood, being an element of the earth, grounds the energy of the cards and offers a solid protective barrier. You may want to choose a box made from a specific type of wood, like cedar or oak, for their unique, energetic properties. You can also adorn the box with protective symbols like the pentagram or triquetra.

Dedicated tarot bags can be made from any material like velvet, silk, satin, or cotton. They're a portable and convenient way to store your deck and endless pattern choices. These bags can be easily purchased or handcrafted, allowing for personalization. Drawstring closures ensure that the cards remain secure. You can line your tarot bag with mugwort for psychic energy blessings and place moonstone beads on the drawstring ends for magical enhancement.

If you're lucky enough to have a dedicated spiritual space or altar at home, placing your tarot deck there can be both magical and symbolic. This method ensures that the deck is treated with reverence, always in a sacred space, and ready for use. When stored alongside other spiritual tools or books, the tarot deck is continuously charged with positive and sacred energies. You're also more likely to use the deck when it's out and seen regularly.

Other modern ways to store your tarot decks include pencil cases, jewelry boxes, tins and even makeup bags. While these lack the traditional or mystical appeal of other storage methods, they make up for it in practicality and durability.

Remember, the best storage method for your tarot deck is one that you're going to use, is within your budget, and resonates with you.

Shuffling and Selecting Cards

There is no one right way to shuffle your tarot cards. Tarot decks come in different sizes and shapes, and we all have various sizes of hands. You can riffle shuffle, overhand shuffle, and even move your cards around on a table like you're Daniel from *The Karate Kid*, wax-on, wax-off style. Allow the time it takes to shuffle the tarot cards as a way to center yourself, focus on your intention and add magic to your tarot readings.

Some practitioners can't shuffle their cards at all; however, this doesn't mean that your reading is going to be less powerful and meaningful than those who shuffle their cards as if they work at the local casino. Allow your energy and intention to lead you to the cards you need for reading if you aren't able to shuffle the cards. Your intuition always knows the message that needs to be delivered.

Many tarot readers will cut the deck of cards after they shuffle them and select the cards from the top pile. It's said that if you do this with your left hand, you're using the more intuitive side of your brain. Some tarot readers will shuffle the deck each time they select a card in a spread. Other techniques include cutting the deck into three piles and asking the querent (the person the tarot reading is for) to pick the pile they feel the most drawn to and select the cards from the top of that pile. Other readers will fan out the tarot cards on the table, run their hands over them, and stop when they're energetically drawn to a card. Try different methods of shuffling until you find one that feels right for you.

There are techniques you can carry out while shuffling your tarot cards to imbue them with magic and intention. This is a perfect way to bind your tarot cards together with your magical spellcasting. Shuffling the cards is a magical action, after all.

This first method uses intentional breath and visualization. This method allows you to become centered before your readings, work your psychic muscles and put intentional energy into your cards. Hold your tarot deck in your hands and place it close to your heart chakra. Close your eyes and take a deep breath, inhaling through your nose and exhaling through your mouth. As you breathe, visualize a pure white, or gold light emanating from the universe, entering the crown of your head through your crown chakra, and flowing down to envelop your entire body. You can see this as a fountain, waterfall, or a sprinkle. As you continue to breathe, imagine this light concentrating in your heart chakra, then flowing down your arms and into your tarot deck in your hands. Slowly open your eyes and start to shuffle your deck. As you shuffle your cards, feel them being infused with this magical energy. When you want to work with abundance and prosperity magic, feel the light turn to a brilliant, healthy green or gold. Turn this energy into loving pink energy when you want to work with love and friendship magic and readings. Silver is a perfect light for protection. Orange and yellow are wonderful for courage and energy boosts. Universal white or gold light can be used for all workings. When you're ready, open your eyes and start your tarot reading and tarot spell.

This second method uses affirmations to add magic to your tarot cards. This is an excellent way for people who struggle to visualize things to add their intention to the deck. Before you begin, create a custom affirmation that aligns with the magical purpose of your reading. This could be something like, "I bless and align my cards with prosperity; may my work bring me the success I desire," or "May the Divine energies of love and truth bring me the answers I seek and aid me in manifesting my magic." Hold your tarot deck in your hands, close your eyes, and bring your awareness to your center, your breath, your cards, and the energy that connects it all. Begin shuffling your cards while slowly and deliberately repeating your affirmation out loud or silently. If you can visualize the words' energy flowing into the cards as well, do this. If not, feel it working as you speak the words of power. Continue this process until you feel intuitively drawn to stop shuffling and speaking the affirmation. When you're ready, you can open your eyes and start your tarot reading and magical working.

Both of these methods aim to infuse the act of shuffling with intention and magical energy, ensuring that your tarot cards are aligned with your chosen purpose. By incorporating these practices, you're preparing the cards for reading and deepening your connection with the deck and the energies it channels.

My Tarot Reading Rituals

These are the ritual steps I take in my tarot readings, some before and some after I carry out any tarot readings for myself or my clients. Of course, if I'm reading the tarot out at a café or other public space, I may carry out an abridged version of this ritual. Adapt this and use it if you feel drawn to it.

My first step is to select the tarot deck and crystals I feel drawn to that day. I spray my aura with a cleansing aura spray and then anoint my wrists with psychic powers oil. Next, I light a white candle, close my eyes, and breathe while holding the intention I want to create for the session. I fall into a semi-meditative state and open my energy to my higher self and spirit guides. I recite my devotion to welcome spirit guides. At this point I can see in my mind's eye that my energy is protected and that I'm connected to my guides. Finally, I open my eyes and begin my session. I keep my white candle lit throughout my reading sessions and will carry out any readings I wish to do back to back or with short breaks in between.

To close out my tarot reading sessions, I place my tarot cards back in a single pile and put them back on my altar with a crystal on top to cleanse them. I spray my aura with the cleansing spray. To bring my energy back into my body, I close my eyes and I thank my spirit guides in this space for assisting me in my tarot readings. I open my eyes, snuff out the candle, then drink a full glass of water and have something grounding to eat.

Chapter 3
The Major Arcana

The major arcana represent the central theme and energy of a reading. Each card is not merely an image but a reflection of universal archetypes, tapping into the collective unconscious to reveal significant truths about our life paths, challenges, and opportunities. When these cards appear in a reading, they suggest you'll soon encounter pivotal moments and life lessons. The archetypes found in the major arcana touch the lives of people all around the globe, no matter their geographical location, religious or spiritual beliefs, or goals in life. The major arcana shed light on the big energies at play in a querent's life, and the minor arcana is the everyday embodiment of those energies. When working with the major arcana cards, notice the colors, symbols, and items that stand out; each detail can unveil aspects of your journey. Ask yourself: What energies are these elements introducing into the reading? What do the specific symbols or colors that resonate with me signify in the context of my current experiences or query? These reflective questions can deepen your understanding of the wisdom of the cards, guiding you toward a more profound awareness of your path and power in life.

0
The Fool

Key concepts: Beginnings, folly, potential, opportunities

The Fool is a card of pure potential. It evokes the feeling in your stomach of excitement and a little trepidation. It's the card of new beginnings and journeys in life on all levels. It can manifest in many ways. A new career, a new relationship, or undertaking a new spiritual path. Numbered 0, it's a perfect circle, never ending and never beginning. The Fool is carefree and unmarked by life experiences, both positive and negative. This is a card for following your curiosity and intuition. Fearlessness is a companion of the Fool. They don't see any risks or danger, allowing them to do wonderful things, even if it's a little foolish.

Take the Leap Spread

The tarot spread for the Fool is perfect for when you're on the brink of a significant change in your life. When you're going to make a decision, others may wonder what you're thinking; you may even wonder what you're thinking. Everyone gets cold feet; however, sometimes you have to feel the fear and do it anyway.

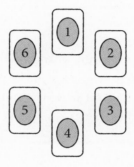

1. Am I being foolish?
2. What do I need to consider before I leap?
3. How can I be more fearless?
4. What limiting beliefs will hold me back in this new adventure?
5. What impulses need taming on this journey?
6. What's the next action to take before I leap?

Have Faith Charm

The Have Faith Charm has been created to carry the Fool's open energy throughout your life. The magical charm is meant to be worn anytime you're about to undergo a significant life-altering change, a new cycle in life, or take a risk.

Best time to cast: New Moon

You will need

- Acrylic paint pens in white and gold
- A small river stone

Take your white paint pen and make a rose design on the stone. The white rose often shown in the Fool tarot card represents faith, innocence, and purity. Then, take the gold paint pen and outline the rose with gold. As you paint the stone, repeat this chant: "The faith I have, I have in me, I've got this, so mote it be!"

Let the stone dry, then place it on your altar or somewhere where you'll see it often to boost your faith in yourself.

Art Magic Tip

Acrylic paint pens have been a game changer for me when it comes to my art magic. They're easy to store, come in many tip styles, and are way less messy. Think of them as magical art wands! You can use acrylic paints if you don't have access to these pens.

1
The Magician

Key concepts: Manifestation, action, resources, skills

In many tarot decks, the Magician is shown with the tools required to explore the journeys of each of the minor arcana suits in the deck. A chalice may be shown for the suit of the Cups, a sword for the suit of the Swords, a wand for the suit of the Wands, and a pentacle for the suit of the Pentacles.

This card shows you that you're born with everything you need: all of the tools and all of the power to manifest real change. What we do with that is an entirely individual story.

The Magician is a reminder that we must tackle issues and situations from different angles. Still, ultimately, we have to use the skills and tools, even the intangible ones, to our advantage in order to make decisions and take the appropriate action. When we do this, we're able to bring things into the material realm. The Magician reminds us that we can co-create our lives with the cosmos.

How Can I Tackle This Issue? Spread

The tarot spread for the Magician has been created to be used when you have an issue or situation in front of you that is a real head-scratcher. It can be really debilitating to face an issue where you have no idea where to start. Before you throw your hands up, declare "Fuck this," and do something rash, spend some time with this tarot spread and arm yourself with information to get the job done and done right!

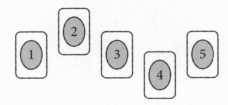

1. What haven't I considered when it comes to this issue?
2. What are the best tools for the job?
3. What allies should I connect with for success?
4. What do I need to avoid when taking action?
5. What energy do I need to embody to achieve positive results?

Empowerment Tea Spell

The Magician spell is an empowerment spell. It is ideal when you're looking at undertaking something you feel you don't have the energy for. This spell can be done at any time for an instant boost of motivation and empowerment for day-to-day tasks or for more significant undertakings that feel overwhelming. The tea is also delicious and good for you.

Best time to cast: Anytime

You will need

- Yellow pen
- Small piece of paper
- A knife
- One lemon
- Mug of hot water
- One tablespoon of grated fresh or dried ginger
- A small piece of tumbled citrine

Using the yellow pen, write down the task or project that you don't have the energy for on a small piece of paper. As you write this, feel your apathy pour out of you into the writing, transferring this stagnant energy into the words and onto the paper. Slice your lemon into circles and place them into the water with ginger. Allow the tea to steep. Fold the piece of paper and place it under the mug of tea. Hold the piece of citrine in your hand and say, "As I hold this piece of sunshine, joy, and energy and drink this elixir of empowerment, may I have all I need to complete this task. As I will it, so mote it be!"

Drink the empowerment tea while holding the citrine. When you have finished the spell, place the citrine in your pocket or put it somewhere close by as you complete your tasks. Or you can carry it in your pocket for a boost of energy when you feel yourself losing motivation.

Magical Spice Law

The spicy root of ginger is associated with the planet Mars and the element of fire. It will inject passion and energy into your life and get you moving!

2

The High Priestess

Key concepts: Intuition, mystery, the subconscious, passiveness

The High Priestess sits in the middle of two black and white pillars. She is the spiritual embodiment of the liminal wisdom that lives in the in-between places. When you look at the card of the High Priestess, you'll see that the card's symbols all connect to her otherworldly energy. The Moon is a symbol of intuition and wisdom; she has a scroll of knowledge on her lap and pomegranates behind her.

This card asks you to lean into your spiritual development, get comfortable with silence, and be in your own space. Intuitive messages require space and quiet in order to be heard. When there is space created for your inner knowing to present itself, that's when you can really begin to access your deep well of wisdom.

Spiritual Development Spread

The High Priestess's tarot spread is her calling to you to sit by her side and listen to your intuition when it comes to the path forward in your spiritual development. We all get stuck sometimes and don't know what we don't know. As the keeper of many secrets, mysteries, and ancient knowledge, the High Priestess is the perfect teacher to guide you on your way.

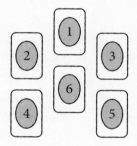

1. How can I move toward making peace with the past?
2. How is my intuition trying to speak to me?
3. What is the best way to get to know myself better?
4. How can I honor my inner wisdom today?
5. What mysteries are being presented to me?
6. How can I embody the archetype of the High Priestess more in my life?

Psychic Powers Anointing Oil

You'll create psychic power anointing oil with the High Priestess, which you can use anytime you do tarot readings, divination practices of all kinds, rituals and meditation.

Best time to cast: **Anytime**

You will need

- Small glass bottle with a lid (a used essential oil bottle is perfect)
- A small funnel
- Carrier oil, such as apricot kernel oil

- A small amethyst or clear quartz stone (must be able to fit in the bottle)
- A pinch of dried mugwort
- A pinch of dried yarrow
- A pinch of dried wood betony

All of these ingredients need to fit into your bottle, so please adjust the quantities to fit the size of your bottle.

Take your bottle and place the funnel in the opening. Pour the carrier oil into the bottle and fill it two-thirds of the way. Take the funnel out. Place the small crystal in the bottle. The crystal is used to amplify the oil's power. Place your herbs in the bottle. Secure the lid of the bottle and give it a shake. Hold the bottle in your hands and take a moment to thank the plant and crystal spirits for their gifts of psychic powers. Let the oil sit for three days before you use it. The longer you leave it, the more powerful it will become. It's recommended that you store this oil out of direct sunlight.

Magical Tools

Anointing oil, also called holy oil, empowers or blesses a person or object with the intended energy. Anointing oil can be used on candles, oil burners, and spells. It can be placed on a person's wrists and temples before meditations, spells, readings, and rituals. Always test the oil before placing a healthy amount on your wrist to ensure you won't have an allergic reaction to one of the ingredients.

3
The Empress

Key concepts: Nature, fertility, creativity, abundance

The Empress holds the energy of the Great Mother. This is on the grand scale of Mother Nature and also from the mother that gives us life. This card represents the lushness of nature and fertility but also the harshness of her awe-inspiring power. The Empress card represents all creative endeavors and projects and the effort needed to nurture something into being.

Healing the Mother Wound Spread

The mother wound in modern psychology refers to the emotional and psychological pain experienced by individuals, often resulting from a strained or dysfunctional relationship with their mother. This wound can manifest through feelings of inadequacy, low self-esteem, and a deep-seated sense of unworthiness. Healing your mother wound will take time. It's not something that can be done in a straightforward step. You may need to use this tarot spread more than once throughout your healing journey with the mother wound. I also recommend that you get some support with your mother wound if this is a core wound in your life. Supportive and loving energy is connected to the Empress, so make sure you set yourself up for success.

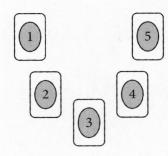

1. How can I honor myself during this process?
2. What pain needs expressing?
3. What does my inner child need from me now?
4. How can I release my resentment?
5. How can I start to forgive my mother?

Fertility Spell

Fertility spells are not meant to be a replacement for fertility treatments or proper medical assistance. Anyone who tells you that they can guarantee a pregnancy with a magical spell is trying to sell you a lie. Carrying out this fertility spell for yourself is more likely to be successful than having someone else cast the spell for you or doing it for someone else.

Best time to cast: Three nights before the Full Moon

You will need

- Small red silk pouch
- A long piece of red cord
- A small shell
- A small, tumbled garnet
- Some coconut shavings
- A couple of drops of rose oil or dried rose petals

All of these ingredients need to fit into your pouch. Please adjust the quantities to fit the size of your pouch.

Put the ingredients into the pouch. Seal it by either tying knots in the cord or hand sewing it shut. When this is complete, hold the pouch to your reproductive organs and say, "Red for vitality and life, a shell for the sea, garnet for strength, pregnant I'll soon be. Coconut sacred to Sri, roses for love, we call you, dear soul, come to us from above."

Take some time to feel your energy going into the pouch and visualize your reproductive organs becoming fertile. You want to wear this pouch either close to your heart chakra or by your hips if you're trying to conceive. If you're unable to do this, place the bag under your pillow and make sure it's closed while you're having procreational sex or fertilizing an egg. Wear this pouch until you receive confirmation of pregnancy.

4
The Emperor

Key concepts: Stability, structure, authority, protection

Now, we meet the Great Father archetype of the tarot. In its positive energy, this card is connected to leadership, protection, and stability. These are all wonderful energies to help people achieve great things in life. They're a strong presence that helps bring structure to their endeavors. When they're in their destructive or absent energy, they can be overbearing and unyielding. However, the Emperor will meet any challenge head-on and with all that they have.

Healing the Father Wound Spread

The father wound in modern psychology refers to the emotional and psychological distress caused by an absent, neglectful, or abusive father. Father wounds may manifest in a number of ways, but the most common are feelings of rejection, abandonment, and a deep-seated sense of not being good enough. Just like the mother wound, it takes time to heal. The benefit of tackling these parental wounds is that the next generation doesn't have to experience the same cycles and trauma that you did. Even recognizing that there is an issue is a start, so be gentle with yourself when healing the father wound and become the protector and leader you needed when you were younger.

1. How can I protect my inner child?
2. How can I show up for myself more?
3. How can I be kinder to myself?
4. How can I heal my relationship with authority figures?
5. How can I start to forgive my father?

Strong Constitution Spell

The spell offering for the Emperor embraces one of the positive aspects of the card and of its energy within all of us. Constitution is what we're made of. It's the structure of ourselves, and when that's strong, everything in our lives benefits. Think of this spell as a way to reinforce your energy foundations so that the decisions you make are made from a place of security and personal power.

Best time to cast: **Midday**

You will need

- A printed photo of yourself
- Yellow and orange watercolor paint
- Paint brushes and water

If you don't have a full photo of yourself, you can draw an outline of a person and write your full name and date of birth on it as a substitute. The photo should be one of your whole body, as the spell is meant to bring strength to every part of your body.

Take the photo or cutout of yourself and paint it yellow with the paint. While it dries, chant, "Strength, energy, solid foundation, my makeup, my will is unshaken."

After it's dry, paint the zodiac sign of Aries over the top in bold orange. When you've completed that, say, "As I will it, with the power of Aries, so shall it be!"

Allow this to dry thoroughly and place it somewhere that it will see the daily Sun.

Magical Timing Law

Not all spells are best cast under the light of the Moon. Some are better to be done during the day, especially for spells for strength and energy. If you can, do this spell outside under the Sun, as the Sun's consistent shine boosts these types of spells.

5
The Hierophant

Key concepts: Institutions, teaching, wisdom, tradition

Any person or organization you come into contact with has a deep connection with the Hierophant. This card represents the religions of the world, our ancestry, and all of the teachers we come in contact with throughout our lives. In its positive aspect, the Hierophant imparts wisdom and provides social approval. In the destructive aspect, the sheer power of governments and institutions can be cages and terrible oppressors. The good news is that you get to choose what traditions and institutions you support and are part of.

Healing the Institutional Wound Spread

The institutional wounds we see in society are deep. This has been reflected in the feedback I've received from students when they reflect on the Hierophant. Many people struggle with experiences in religious groups that feel isolating and harmful. This wound can also show up as being left behind in education systems and techniques. Wounds from religion, education systems, family and government often go back many generations. The tarot spread offered for the Hierophant can aid you in coming back to yourself and your inner knowledge instead of what outside influences have led you to believe.

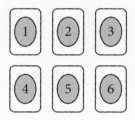

1. How can I embrace my individuality more?
2. What beliefs about myself do I need to release?
3. What beliefs about myself do I need to embrace?
4. What superpower of mine was being repressed?
5. How can I transform my connection with my inner knowledge?
6. What ally can I partner with to help my healing?

Spiritual Guidance Spell

The spell offering for this card is one of the ways you can build a connection with your spirit guides. Not everyone has the ability to meditate and see their guides. Using this spell can be a way to interact with and get messages from them in a direct fashion. You can do this anywhere! Look out for synchronicities when you've cast this spell. You may see symbols or art throughout the day that link back to your messages.

Best time to cast: Anytime

You will need

- Your phone or a radio

Take some time to bring your energy back to yourself. You can close your eyes and feel your thoughts and energy coming back to you with every inhalation. When you're ready and feel centered enough, say, "Spirit guides, I need a sign, I need a message, some help divine. Deliver it to me, and may it be clear, the wisdom I'm seeking will now appear."

Now, take your phone, open your favorite listening app, go to a random playlist, and hit shuffle. Listen to the song that comes up, even if it's not your favorite song. Close your eyes and listen to the lyrics. Feel them in your body. This is your message when you feel a change in your vibration or when a lyric resonates with you. If for some reason you stumble across songs of self-harm or harming others (because there is music like that out there), redo the process.

6
The Lovers

Key concepts: Relationships, love, community, choice

The Lovers card is, of course, connected to romantic relationships and connections of the heart. Unions that leave a lasting impression on your soul and even sexy summer flings are all within the realm of the Lovers card. This is also a card of values and all of the ingredients that make relationships work outside of sexual attraction. Important lessons are offered through these connections and partnerships. They can be the sweetest thing you've ever known, down to the most profound pain you'll ever experience.

What Love Means to Me Spread

When building a lasting relationship, knowing what you need in a relationship and what's truly important is key. Knowing what love means to you ensures that you'll attract the right partnerships into your life. If you want to marry for money and status, do your thing, but own that decision and path for yourself. If you'd rather be single and have deep friendships, that works too. The Lovers tarot spread is here to help you understand yourself and your love values so you can love who and how you want.

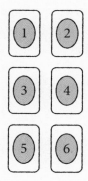

1. What kind of love is good for me right now?
2. What outdated beliefs do I have about love?
3. What kind of relationship am I currently attracting?
4. What kind of love am I craving right now?
5. What gifts do I bring to my romantic relationships?
6. How can I attract my ideal romantic partner?

Come and Light My Fire Spell

The tarot spell for the Lovers is a feisty one. It's the spell you want to cast when you need someone in between the sheets or on top of them. You can use this to call in a new lover or reignite passion in your relationships. Never underestimate the power of communication in your relationships and the need for connection outside the bedroom.

Best time to cast: New to Full Moon

You will need

- An empty and clean oyster shell
- Candle carving tool or toothpick
- Three red or white tealight candles
- Lighter or match

Place the clean oyster shell with its cradle facing upward. Using your tool, carve your name on the face of the candle. Light the candle and say, "Goddess of passion, send me a lover, give a night of heat and pleasure on and under the covers. May they know all my zones and get me off too; may they be safe to engage with and uncomplicated too!" Allow the candle to burn completely. Do this spell at least three days in a row. You can use the same oyster shell each time but burn a new candle each day.

7
The Chariot

Key concepts: Willpower, control, freedom, ambition

The Chariot is the tarot card of discipline and what it takes to overcome life's obstacles. While this is a card for obtaining success, it doesn't come without effort and work. The Chariot card will test your skills and abilities. You have to choose the right tools, protection, and modalities to succeed, and the charioteer knows this. There is freedom with the Chariot. You can go where you want and do what you want. That also means that you're on your own. You'll soon find out what you're made of when you have to rely on yourself and own your decisions.

Torn Between Two Decisions Spread

A common symbol in the Chariot is the two sphinxes pulling the chariot. Depending on the deck theme, some decks will have horses or other beings. These represent the opposing forces at play when we are working on a goal. It could represent the right or left side of the brain, practical decisions versus risk, or two roads to lead the Chariot down. The tarot spread for this card will help you assess which road is best suited for you.

For this spread, you'll pick cards one and two before you shuffle the deck and carry out the rest of the reading. Go through your tarot deck, pick a card that represents your first option, and place it in position one. Then, do the same for position two. You may use the keywords associated with the cards to make your choice, or you may feel intuitively what card best represents your choices.

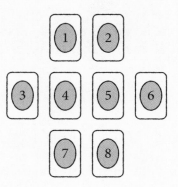

1. The card that represents the first option I am looking to make.
2. The card that represents the second option I'm looking to make.

Then, shuffle your cards while thinking about the first option. You can talk out loud about the option or look at the tarot card you chose to represent it. When you're ready, cut the deck and place cards three, four, and five in their positions.

Shuffle your cards with the remainder of the deck while thinking about the second option. You can talk out loud about the option or look at the tarot card you chose to represent it. When you're ready, cut the deck and place cards six, seven, and eight in their positions.

You now have a line of cards for each option that you can interpret and get guidance for which is the best way to go.

3. What are the potential obstacles and challenges of the first option?
4. What are the benefits and successes of the first option?
5. What is the most likely outcome if I choose the first option?
6. What are the obstacles and challenges of the second option?
7. What are the benefits and successes of the second option?
8. What is the most likely outcome if I choose the second option?

Car Protection Spell

The Chariot often represents modes of transportation in readings, so the spell for the Chariot is a car protection spell. This protection spell will ensure that you're protected while you drive and will keep your car hidden from people who may want to break into it. It can also protect your vehicle from being dinged by other drivers in car parks and all sorts of unwanted situations on and off the road.

Best time to cast: Full Moon

You will need

- A pencil and eraser
- A thin wooden disk
- A black permanent marker
- Three drops of rosemary, clove or eucalyptus oil

Using your pencil, copy the car protection sigil onto your wooden disk. On the back of your wooden disk put your car's license plate number. Then, go over the protective sigil and plate number with the permanent marker.

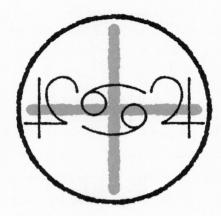

Drop three drops of your chosen protective oil and allow it to soak in. You don't want to drench the disk in oil. It's not safe. Place your hand just above the sigil and pour universal energy into it, like you're giving the sigil Reiki. Then say, "Activate this protective sigil for my car and all that is carried in it. From this day, my car is protected from any harmful people and incidents. As I will it, so mote it be." Place the protection sigil disk in your car's glove compartment and leave it there.

Magical Spell Tip

It's completely acceptable to do this protective sigil on a piece of paper. It will work. I like the durability of doing this on something like a thin wooden disk. It'll last longer and is less likely to get damaged or lost in the car. Blank wooden Christmas ornaments are perfect for this spell.

8
Strength

Key concepts: Force, strength, confidence, bravery

Not all strength is a show of brute force. Some power is silent and gentle and is just as effective. The figure in the Strength card is often seen taming a wild beast. They're still following through even if they're frightened by what may happen. This card represents having courage and self-confidence and not giving in to fear or taking the easy way out. This card shows how people use the power they have in the world. Are they kind and compassionate, or do they want to show off their prowess to impress everyone?

Force Spread

When faced with opposition, the tarot spread for Strength is what you need to resolve it. Some situations will call for you to be patient and understanding; other times, you must embrace your inner wrecking ball. It's always good to know you have options so you can tackle what's in front of you confidently and well-informed.

1. What is the real challenge I'm facing?
2. What is the virtue that's being tested?
3. Where do I need to show patience?
4. What are the hidden motivations or agendas?
5. What is the outcome if gentleness is used?
6. What is the outcome if force is shown?

Protect My Child Spell

There's nothing like the protective capabilities of a parent. I know there is pretty much nothing I wouldn't do to protect my child. The Strength spell can go with your child anywhere and is especially effective when they're attending school. Children can be vicious, and parents can't be everywhere all at once. This spell has been simplified, with one of the components being a ready-made orange coin pouch. If you're crafty, you can make one for your child from scratch. A fabric or a design with a lion or lioness on it will add more strength to the energy of this spell.

Best time to cast: **Full Moon**

You will need

- A small orange coin purse
- A lemniscate (infinity symbol) charm
- A lion or lioness charm
- A tumbled piece of smoky quartz
- A tumbled piece of garnet

Hold the orange coin purse to your heart and feel the love and protection you have for your child pour into the purse. Add the charms and tumbled stones and zip the bag up. Say, "Invisible from harm, (your child's name) will be today and every day. Protected and loved at all times, at school, home, or away. So mote it be." Place the protective coin purse in your child's school bag, travel backpack, or favorite bag. Use a keychain attachment so it doesn't fall out or get lost by the typical wear and tear a child's bag goes through during the day. Often, there are small loops inside backpacks that you can secure it to.

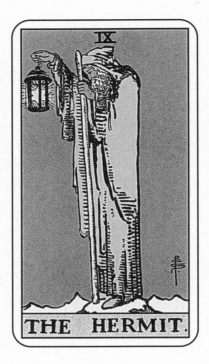

9
The Hermit

Key concepts: Contemplation, introspection, solitude, guidance

The Hermit isn't afraid of spending time alone. Most of the time, they seek it out as they're fully aware that their inner voice can be heard better in solitude. This is the card of meditation, self-reflection, journaling, pathworking, and all other contemplative practices. The Hermit wants us to find ourselves and look for answers within, sometimes in places that other people are too afraid to look. The Hermit is a reminder that even when we're alone, we have a team of guides beside us, and we're never cut off from the Divine source.

Message from My Spirit Guides Spread

The tarot spread for the Hermit is designed for you to gain clear messages from your spirit guides. The tarot is a perfect tool for working with spirit guides. It's like having a phone line to spirit, with a road map to follow. The cards show you directly what you need to know. They also work your psychic muscles to gain deeper insight into your readings. You don't have to know your spirit guides specifically to use this tarot spread. It may be the first time you've ever connected with them. Like any relationship, forming a bond may take some time, and this is an excellent place to start.

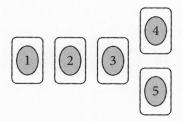

1. What spirit guide wants to work with me?

2. What is the reason this guide has connected with me?

3. How will this spirit guide help me?

4. What is the message my spirit guide needs to share?

5. What is the healing/action my spirit guide wants me to embrace?

Wax Scrying Spell

One of the key symbols in the Hermit card is the lantern the figure is holding. It represents ideas, inner light, and the power of wisdom and knowledge. The spell for this card is a form of divination using candle wax. You can use any type of candle where the wax will pool enough so you can pour it. This is a fun witchy activity to do with friends as you can help each other interpret the wax shapes.

Best time to cast: Anytime

You will need

- The Hermit tarot card
- Tealight candle or votive
- Lighter or match
- Journal or paper and pen
- Cup of water
- Paper towel

Place your chosen Hermit card in front of you and light your candle. Say, "May the light of the Hermit shine and may clear messages soon be mine." Write in the journal or on the paper the question you want the answer to. Allow the candle wax to pool. When you have enough melted wax, pour it into the cup of water. Allow the wax to become solid again. Gently take the wax out of the water and dry it with a paper towel. Turn the wax form around and observe it from many angles. Write whatever comes to you in your journal or on the piece of paper. Don't overthink it. Just allow whatever comes to your mind to flow to the page while you're meditating on the wax. You may see numbers, animals, tools, or magical symbols in the wax. Search for any symbols you're not sure of after your session. If you're not sure why you've received a symbol or message, sleep on it or come back to it later. We aren't always sure what messages from spirit mean in the moment.

10
Wheel of Fortune

Key concepts: Cycles, change, luck, chance

The Wheel of Fortune reminds us that nothing in the world stays the same, and all circumstances change. There are times when you feel on top of the world (wheel) and other times when you'd rather not venture out of the safety of your bed because life sucks. This is a card of the seasons and cycles in our lives. Whether you believe in destiny or chaos theory, the Wheel of Fortune has a place in both because we're constantly changing and making choices in our daily lives.

Get Lucky Spread

The Get Lucky Spread can help you get into alignment with the flow of Lady Luck. It can help you align yourself to be in the right place at the right time for a life-altering job opportunity or to meet the person of your dreams. This is also a powerful spread if you've felt like your luck has been shitty lately. Empower yourself with the cards to do something about getting back into luck's good graces.

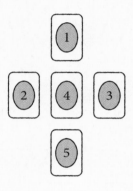

1. What is causing my bad luck?
2. What will attract good luck?
3. Where will I find something lucky?
4. What can I do to stop attracting bad luck?
5. How can I embrace Lady Luck's energy in my life?

Good Luck Spell

The Good Luck Spell is an easy talisman you can use to be in step with lucky energies throughout the day. Anyone who's seen *Deadpool 2* and Domino's powers knows just how formidable good luck can be. When you've completed this talisman, try to be in a place of flow rather than overthinking things. Allow for change and flexibility to be part of how you move in the world so you can adapt when good things happen and move out of the way when lousy luck heads your way.

Best time to cast: Anytime

You will need

- Green shoelaces or hemp cord
- A four-leaf clover charm
- A small bell

Replace your shoelaces with the green ones, and on one of your shoes, place the four-leaf clover charm and the bell at the bottom lace of the shoe. Every time you walk and the bell rings, you'll bring yourself good luck. If you don't wear shoes with laces, make an anklet with green hemp string, the charm, and the bell. Don't take off the anklet; wear it until it breaks off.

11
Justice

Key concepts: Cause and effect, truth, fairness, law

Justice doesn't care that life's not fair sometimes; it's concerned with what is. This is a card of consequences and truth. At times, that's harsh, and other times, it feels like a welcoming win. Justice will balance the scales; it just may not be in the way you're expecting. In a more muggle sense, this card is connected to the law, legal matters, and life lessons, big and small.

You Get What You Give Spread

If you want to know if someone is going to get the energy they deserve for their actions, it's time to use the tarot spread for Justice. This spread is perfect for any situation you've had with a person that feels like it's connected to a past life or a soul contract. You'll also be able to understand your own cosmic energy and lessons so that you don't have to go through it all over again.

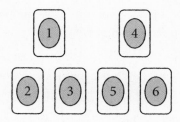

1. What is the universal truth of the situation?
2. What is the cosmic lesson of my current situation?
3. What is the energy flowing to me?
4. What is the cosmic lesson of the other party?
5. What is the energy flowing to them?
6. How can I avoid this happening again?

Swift Justice Spell

The spell for the Justice tarot card comes with a warning. Don't cast it unless you're ready to face your own cause-and-effect energy. People can become blinded by wanting personal justice without considering their actions and what effect those actions may cause. As long as you can accept the consequences of your actions, cast away and bring swift justice to your situation.

Best time to cast: Full Moon

You will need

- Black Sharpie marker
- Six nails
- Hammer
- A small, cut-off piece of wood

With a black Sharpie marker, write the full name and date of birth of the person you want to see come to justice on the piece of wood. While you hammer the nails into the piece of wood, say the following incantation.

Nail of one, your karmic comeuppance has begun

Nail of two, I'm done with you

Nail of three, I'm completely set free

Nail of four, dodging justice no more

Nail of five, swift justice has arrived

Nail of six, the universe sees through your tricks

May this spell not reverse and only bring the justice that's owed

So shall it be

Take the piece of wood with the nails off your property and bury it. A place near running water is good as it will keep the flow of justice going. You can also burn it if you have a fireplace. The ashes should later be disposed of off your property.

12
The Hanged Man

Key concepts: New perspectives, surrender,
contemplation, waiting

The Hanged Man's energy can feel constrictive and unpleasant; however, when you embrace the energy of the card and look at it from a different perspective, you start to see the wisdom within. Sometimes in life you need to wait and surrender your control to the universe and let things unfold. This card is a sign from your spirit guides to pause, as a vital piece of information you need hasn't been revealed, and you best wait until you know what you're getting yourself into.

Get Out of Limbo Spread

There's nothing worse than being stuck in limbo. Waiting for a response from someone or the results of a test is an actual trial in patience. Let's face it: humans are not the most patient of creatures. The tarot spread for this card is designed for you to lean into the in-between you're caught in. You may as well use your current circumstances to your advantage rather than letting it drive you bonkers.

1. Why am I stuck?
2. What is the lesson I need to learn while I'm in limbo?
3. What perspective do I need to gain?
4. What sacrifice do I need to make to progress?
5. When is the right time to act?
6. How can I liberate myself?

Bring Change Now Spell

The spell for the Hanged Man is perfect for moving stagnant energy and welcoming positive change. This tarot card embodies stillness, which is needed at times. However, this spell can help things move along when you're done contemplating. Witches use brooms and besoms as magical tools as well as practical ones for cleaning. By sweeping out stale energy, you will create space for change and positivity to come in. Common folklore states that you don't want the broom head to touch the ground if you use it for magical purposes, so store it appropriately.

Best time to cast: New Moon

You will need

- One lucky coin with a hole in it
- Gold ribbon
- Small besom or broom

- Eyebright herb or sprig of the herb while they're in flower

Thread the coin on the gold ribbon and tie it to the broom's cap or heel. Sprinkle some dried eyebright herb on the broom or tie the sprig of the herb to the heel of the broom with the coin. Go to each window sill in your home and doorway and energetically sweep the stagnant energy out the window. You want to ensure the broom doesn't touch the ground, so sweep about an inch off all surfaces. While you sweep, chant, "Away, away, stagnant energy can't stay, change, change, I welcome it today." Keep the broom somewhere in your home or on your altar. You can use the same broom to carry out this spell at any New Moon when you feel the energy in your space start to stagnate again.

13
Death

Key concepts: Transformations, endings, resolution, letting go

Death is one of the "big, bad" cards in the tarot deck, as often shown in B-grade horror movies with tarot cards in it. It's not surprising death is the great unknown. It is permanent, is inevitable, and represents all things we resist deep down in our wiring. Death, however, is a liberator and the great equalizer. The card represents accepting what is and letting go of what is no longer serving us. All life-altering changes, from the ending of a significant relationship to the death of a loved one, are connected to this card.

Mediumship Spread

If you don't believe in an afterlife, you may never use the mediumship tarot spread, and that's okay. Mediumship readings can bring closure and peace to those who've lost a loved one. It can take time to develop your skills as a medium, so don't fret if you don't get any clear messages from someone on the other side right away. It's also recommended that you have a photo of the person you want to reach with you when you're carrying out this reading. This will ensure that you're bringing the right spirit to the reading.

For the first card in this tarot spread, take your deck and select the tarot card that represents the spirit of the loved one you would like to connect with. Many readers use the tarot court cards for this purpose. You don't need to know anything about the cards; select the card that feels intuitively like the passed loved one. Place that in the first position in the spread. Then, shuffle the rest of the deck and carry out the rest of the reading as you normally would.

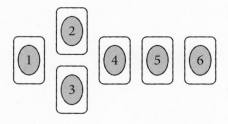

1. The card that represents the spirit.

2. What is the message the spirit has for me?

3. What is the message the spirit has for my family?

4. What advice do they want to share with me?

5. How can I best follow through with the advice?

6. How can I best honor this spirit?

Tarot Reading Tip

The Death card doesn't immediately mean physical death. It's important to know; however, there are times when it does. Death is a part of life. I don't recommend predicting people's deaths unless you have the necessary skills.

Communicate with a Lost Loved One

The communication spell for this card is a beautiful way to connect with a loved one who's passed. If you don't have a personal item from the person, you can bring something you know they loved in life to the spell. Their favorite beer, flowers, candy, anything that creates a connection. This can be a moving experience, so allow yourself quality time for this spell. If you get nothing, don't fret. The timing may be off, or other factors may be at play, like holding on to expectations or doubt. If nothing comes through, spend this time writing a letter to the person you lost. Communication goes both ways, and so can magic. Channeling can feel a little awkward or silly if you've never done it before. The best thing to do is to lean into it and give it a try without too much judgment.

Best time to cast: Full Moon or Dark Moon

You will need

- A photo of your deceased loved one
- Any piece of jewelry or personal object of theirs you have
- White candle with holder
- Small piece of apophyllite crystal
- Lighter or matches
- Pen and paper

Place the photo and personal items in front of you and next to the white candle with the crystal. Light the candle and focus on the photo of the loved one. Hold the piece of apophyllite in your nondominant hand and keep it there throughout this spell. It'll amplify the connection you make to spirit. Close your eyes and say, "I lovingly welcome you (person's name) to my magical space; I call you in to communicate with you and allow you the opportunity to pass on any messages you wish to share. This is done with the highest love and light, welcome."

Now, place your pen on the page and start to write. Don't overthink things; begin to write as if you're receiving a message from the spirit. Don't stop writing to correct spelling or grammatical mistakes. Some people also prefer to draw rather than write, and that's fine too. When you feel like the message is complete, say thank you and release the spirit. An example of a release could be "Thank you, (person's name), for your presence and sharing your messages with me. Go with love and remembrance. Farewell." Snuff your candle out and place the crystal on your altar. You can then spend some time going over the writing to see if there is anything that resonates with you. If you don't understand the messages, keep it somewhere where you can look at it a few days later and see if anything makes sense. You can always try this process again another time.

14
Temperance

Key concepts: Balance, healing, moderation, tranquillity

The angel on the Temperance card is a welcome image in readings where life has been difficult. It's a sign that a new dawn is coming, and things will start to level out. Temperance comes up in a reading when everyone needs to chill out and embrace being more level-headed. It's a card of healing anything that is out of order. It could literally represent recovering from a medical procedure or flu, healing relationships, or a past trauma. In many cases, healing isn't linear or a one-and-done path. Healing takes time, compassion, bravery, and a holistic approach to bring yourself back into alignment. This is also a card of moderation. Overdoing it in life isn't the way to go when Temperance shows up in a reading, no matter how much fun in the moment it may be to let loose.

Healing Path Spread

The Temperance tarot spread is a way to reflect on your healing journey. It can bring clarity to ways you can support yourself while you mend and identify areas of importance for healing. Sometimes an illness or symptom constantly appearing is masking a deeper wound that would benefit from some attention and healing.

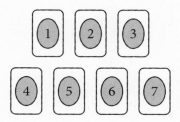

1. What healing do I need to pay attention to right now?
2. How can I physically support this healing?
3. How can I mentally support this healing?
4. How can I emotionally support this healing?
5. Why am I out of alignment?
6. What area of my life needs to be balanced?
7. What support is coming my way for this healing?

Chakra Alignment and Healing Spell

Chakra alignment and healing are perfect when embracing the tarot spell for Temperance. Temperance is a card of blending energy, and when you intentionally use aligned crystals to strengthen your chakras, you're embodying this card. There are so many books and resources on the chakras. The basic information in this grimoire is to help you conduct the spell, but I highly recommend that you work with your chakras throughout your journey, and if you enjoy working with them, continue your education on the system.

Root chakra

- Muladhara chakra
- Color: Red
- Location: Base of the spine

Sacral chakra

- Svadhisthana chakra
- Color: Orange
- Location: Below the navel

Solar plexus chakra

- Manipura chakra
- Color: Yellow
- Location: Just below the ribs

Heart chakra

- Anahata chakra
- Color: Green
- Location: Middle of the chest at heart height

Throat chakra

- Vishuddha chakra
- Color: Blue
- Location: Base of the throat

Third eye chakra

- Ajna chakra
- Color: Indigo/purple
- Location: Between the brows

Crown chakra

- Sahasrara chakra
- Color: Violet/magenta
- Location: Crown of head

Best time to cast: Anytime

You will need

A tumbled crystal for each of seven of the main chakras. I've provided the following suggestions:

- Root chakra: red jasper, bloodstone, smoky quartz
- Sacral chakra: carnelian, sunstone, orange calcite
- Solar plexus chakra: citrine, pyrite, yellow jasper, or yellow jade
- Heart chakra: green jade, rose quartz, rhodochrosite
- Throat chakra: angelite, sodalite, amazonite
- Third eye chakra: amethyst, lapis lazuli, labradorite
- Crown chakra: clear quartz, selenite, celestite

Lay on your back on your bed and carefully lay the crystals in alignment with your chakras. Once they're in position, close your eyes. Bring your consciousness to your root chakra and the crystal that is there. If you can see the stone in your mind's eye, see its color radiate and bathe that chakra in supportive energy. If you are unable to visualize, feel into it and feel it bathe your chakra with its power. Then, move up to your sacral chakra and complete the same visualization. Take your time with this process. Keep going until you've reached your crown chakra. Before you finish and open your eyes, allow your chakra system some time to be in this space, energized and aligned. Place your crystals in a pouch, and you can use them at any time for this chakra alignment spell. Cleansing your crystals by the light of the Full Moon or in a natural body of water is recommended before you reuse them again.

15
The Devil

Key concepts: Addiction, materialism, temptation, shadow work

Meet the second "big, bad" card of tarot: the Devil. For some, it is the ultimate scapegoat. For others, it is the figure used to exercise control. This is the card of our shadow selves. It represents the things we don't want to advertise on our dating profiles and the suppressed aspects of our being. The

Devil is a mighty card when you're able to lean in and learn the positive aspects of this archetype. Yes, the Devil is connected to all of the vices in life and the trappings of the material world, but we're part of the material world. We can't escape it. By bringing our awareness to the things that try to control us, we start the process of integration and the negative power this card holds starts to wane.

Why Can't I Quit Them? Spread

If you've ever dated someone you know is no good but can't walk away, the tarot spread for the Devil is for you. Perhaps you're entangled with your twin flame (these relationships usually don't live up to the hype) or a past life love with unfinished business. You may just be attracted to the "bad boy/girl/person" archetype because you love the drama that follows in their wake. This spread can help you move toward a better relationship with yourself and, eventually, someone new. The kicker is that you have to want something healthier and be prepared to follow healthy relationship advice when it's offered.

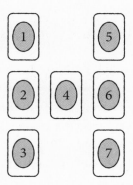

1. Why am I attracted to this person?
2. What is the addictive quality of the relationship?
3. What harm am I doing to myself?
4. What cycle am I playing out?
5. What is the future of this relationship if I stay?
6. What is my romantic future if I leave the relationship?
7. What support do I need to quit this person for good?

Resist Temptation Spell

Everyone has had to resist temptation at some point in their lives. It may have been something small, like not eating another piece of chocolate cake, or it could be something life-altering, like the temptation of an affair. This spell helps you remove yourself from the almost impossible desire to have instant gratification over staying true to yourself and honoring your oaths. If you do end up giving in to temptation, there's no need to criticize yourself or just throw your hands in the air and say, "Fuck it," and give up entirely. Remember that you're only human, and you can get back on track with your next decision.

Best time to cast: **Waning Moon**

You will need

- Small cauldron or flame-resistant container
- Sand
- Red or black candle with holder
- Lighter or matches
- Red pen
- Piece of black paper
- Incense charcoal disk
- Tweezers
- Dried motherwort

Put a small amount of sand in the bottom of the cauldron or flame-safe container. Light your candle, and with the red pen, write down the temptation you're resisting on the piece of black paper. Pick up the charcoal disk with the tweezers and light the disk with the candle's flame. When it's lit, place it on the sand in the cauldron. Sprinkle some of the motherwort on the disk. Allow it to smoke a little. Then, fold up the small piece of paper and place it on the disk. You want the paper to burn along with the herb. As it burns, say, "I no longer desire you, I no longer need you, you're no longer important, I am now freed. So mote it be." Let the candle burn down if possible, and as it burns down, so will your desire for the thing that's tempting you.

Magical Herbal Law

Motherwort herb has the magical properties of protection and being able to counter any harmful magics you may be experiencing.

16
The Tower

Key concepts: Ego, sudden change, upheaval, destruction

The Tower card represents inevitable change without which we would remain chained to illusion and stuck in our own lives. It's usually uncomfortable and unwanted, but some aspects of life are uncomfortable and unwanted. From the sudden shattering of a long-term relationship to disaster striking, this is the card of shit officially hitting the fan. This is also the card of your ego being knocked down a peg or three when life puts you in your place. Nothing will be the same after the Tower's dust settles. It's in these times we genuinely find out what we're made of, but it doesn't make it easier to deal with while we are in the middle of the chaos.

Cope with Sudden Change Spread

This tarot spread is supportive for when you're in those Tower moments of your life. Sitting in a sacred space and making room for your feelings, reactions, and uncertainties can help you get back into your body. It can also feel a lot more productive than panicking. There are well-known steps to accepting change, and you'll experience many feelings during your rebuilding era.

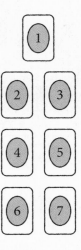

1. What control do I need to let go of?

2. What do I need to do to accept my current situation?

3. What perspective am I being asked to see?

4. What is the secret blessing in this change?

5. What is the foundation from which I can rebuild?

6. What can I do to bring positivity to my situation immediately?

7. What is the best way to find aid?

Shock Absorption Talisman

This shock absorption talisman is really effective. So much so that if the thing breaks, crumbles or gets lost, know that it's done its job. Place them in your cars, briefcases, backpacks, and purses so that they're in locations where you are on the go. In the house, place this one on your altar or near the hearth if you have one. This talisman is created to soak up shock from sudden change so you don't get hit with the full force of it.

Best time to cast: New or Waxing Moon

You will need
- A piece of tumbled malachite stone
- Macrame crystal-holding necklace

If you're a handy DIY person, you can make the macrame crystal holder yourself. If not, you can purchase one. Place the piece of malachite into the macrame crystal necklace. Hold it in your hands and say, "I program you, mineral guardian, to absorb any shock that may come my way, be the first point of contact for unwanted energies." Hang the malachite piece somewhere in your home. Don't be surprised if it smashes, crumbles, or falls and breaks. This means that shock has been absorbed and the spell has been a success. When the crystal has completed its magical work, take the pieces and bury them somewhere off your property.

Crystal Magic Law
Malachite is a stone that's connected to the heart chakra, which needs protection whenever shock is present. It's a protective stone that's said to absorb negative energies. It helps calm the nervous system as well as brings a calming energy to the wearer.

17
The Star

Key concepts: Hope, serenity, renewal, faith

Stars have always guided explorers and philosophers. There are stories, myths and legends connected to the stars all over the world. They teach us lessons, give us hope, and, for some, reinforce faith. These are all aspects that the Star card holds. It's the light in the darkness, our true north. It's a place where you're connected to something bigger than yourself. This card is connected to the faith of all kinds, religious, spiritual, and faith in self. It's a positive card of wishes coming true and a divine or higher power watching over you. If the idea of the universe having your back was a card, this would be it.

Make It Happen Spread

Faith is an integral part of making a dream a reality. If you believe you can, you will find a way. The tarot spread for the Star is a deeper look into that sentiment. Using the tarot as a channel for the card, you're going to get clear indications of what path is best for you to achieve your goal. With any goal attainment or manifestation, be specific about when you want to reach a goal. Write it in detail so you know what you're going after. Of course, the dream doesn't work unless you do, so after you've received your answers from this tarot spread, you have to put it into practice.

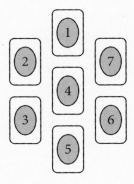

1. What's my real motivation for achieving this goal?

2. What haven't I considered about this goal?

3. What are the potential obstacles I'll face?

4. How do I overcome them?

5. Where do I need to be more accountable?

6. What resources, team, or network do I need to tap into?

7. What will be the impact on my life when I succeed?

Make a Wish Spell

The spell for the Star is a simple general wish spell. This spell has been around for a very long time, and it's so adaptable that you can wish for anything you want. Just like when you blow out your birthday candles and make a wish, the secret is not to share what you wish for with anyone. "To be silent" is a metaphysical tenet to help your magic succeed. Let the universe do its magic and have a little faith that your spell will succeed.

Best time to cast: Full Moon

You will need

- One dried bay leaf
- Gold marker
- Lighter or match
- Shell or cauldron

Under the light of the Full Moon, write your wish on the bay leaf in gold marker. Write it in the present tense, as if your wish has already come true. Light the leaf on fire and drop it into the shell or cauldron, and as you do this, say, "Star above, shining bright, grant this wish, the magic takes flight, bring my dearest wish to me, I summon my desire, so mote it be!" Sprinkle the ashes outside under the Full Moon and let the magic get to work.

18
The Moon

Key concepts: Illusion, fear, dreams, intuition

The Moon is an elusive energy, alluring, magical, and ever-changing. There are always shadows cast when the Moon is out; deep in our subconscious, we fear what's hiding in them. This tarot card reminds us to listen and trust our intuition to guide us through the night. Some fears are warranted, and others are not. Knowing how to tell the difference is a powerful attribute. All psychic abilities are connected to this card; so are our powerful emotions. Often, when this card arrives in a reading, something hidden needs to be found or clarity is elusive. It's the perfect time to listen to your dreams and intuitive wisdom.

Dream Interpretation Spread

The tarot spread for the Moon is extremely helpful when you've had a dream that doesn't make sense. Some dreams are our subconscious replaying events from the day; some dreams are prophetic, and some are you traveling astrally. So much can happen while we dream. I recommend recording your dreams as soon as you wake up. If possible, don't move or speak to anyone; allow your mind some time to recall the details and feelings. Once you start to recall your dreams, it often comes in a wave. I've often woken up in the wee hours of the morning and typed notes about my dreams on my phone so I didn't forget them. It's easier than trying to find a pen and paper in the dark.

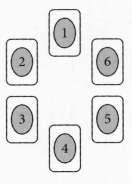

1. What is the reason I had the dream?

2. What is the meaning of the dream?

3. What is the message from my guides in this dream?

4. What has my subconscious mind contributed to this dream?

5. What is the lesson this dream is trying to teach me?

6. What waking action do I need to take on behalf of the dream?

Dream Recall Spell

This Dream Recall Spell is for people who have a hard time recalling and remembering their dreams. Not everyone has the innate ability to remember their dreams. You may only feel certain things about your dreams but fail to recall any images; those feelings are just as valid for dream recall. You may recall messages from your dreams in the form of someone telling you something or a song you heard. The more you acknowledge what you remember in your dreams, even if it's as small and fleeting as a feeling, the more recall you'll have in the future. This spell makes a little pouch for dream recall that you can slip under your pillow or keep by your bed if you move around a lot in your sleep.

Best time to cast: Full Moon

You will need

- A small pouch of fabric for the pillow
- A small tumbled amethyst
- A small tumbled moonstone
- One teaspoon of damiana dried herb
- One teaspoon of dried jasmine flowers
- Two teaspoons of dried mugwort

All of your crystals and herbs need to fit into the pouch, so be aware of that when you pick your crystals. Mix your herbs and place them in your pouch with the crystals. Make sure it is sealed well. You can even sew it shut. You can also use oils if you do not have dried herbs. You will need to put a diffuser bead or fabric inside the pouch for the oils. If you are handy at sewing, you can sew the entire dream pillow.

Before you fall asleep, take your dream pillow or pouch and hold it in your hands. Close your eyes and say to yourself three times, "By the winds of inspiration and memory, I remember my dreams. By the waters of my subconscious and intuition, I remember my dreams. By the intuitive powers of the Moon, I remember my dreams. As I will it, so mote it be." See yourself waking up gently in the morning, recalling your dreams with ease and writing them down. You can now place your pouch or pillow under your regular sleeping pillow or by your bedside and drift off to sleep. Don't forget to place a dream journal or writing tools within arm's reach before you go to bed.

19
The Sun

Key concepts: Positivity, success, vitality, optimism

The Sun is a joyous card that brings life to all it touches. This card often comes up in a reading as a universal cheerleader to encourage you to go out and do your thing. It's a card of authenticity and enthusiasm. When we're in our own power and being true to ourselves, we're embracing the energy of this tarot card. This is also a card for taking action and being an active participant in life. Get outside and feel the Sun on your face. Use the precious life you've been given to do what brings you joy.

Inner Happiness Spread

Being happy is easier on some days than others. Happiness is an emotion that is impermanent, moving and changing. The good news is that even if you're having a bad day, another day will begin within twenty-four hours, bringing the energy of renewal along with it. It's okay not to be okay. The Sun tarot spread is designed to help you find your way back to happiness. Chasing happiness doesn't mean ignoring hard feelings or underlying issues. Working with this tarot spread can help you find gratitude in even the hardest of circumstances.

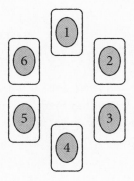

1. What is blocking my happiness?
2. How am I resisting happiness?
3. Where can I find happiness today?
4. What can I do to embrace joy?
5. What does my inner child want me to know?
6. How can I support my inner child's happiness?

Heal Your Inner Child Spell

In a lot of tarot decks, the Sun shows a child on a horse under a bright Sun. This connects the card to inner child work and healing. Healing our inner child is a practice that acknowledges trauma that's occurred in the past and can aid us in moving forward. We get to be the adults we needed as a child to our inner younger selves. This work can be intense if your childhood had significant trauma, so be gentle with yourself and accept professional aid if needed. This spell is a soft first step in healing your inner child. When it comes to choosing the item from your childhood, it doesn't have to be something you had as a child. I would personally use a small Care Bear figure or sticker, as I loved Care Bears as a child and I still do. Select an item that is akin to this for your childhood experience.

Best time to cast: **Full Moon**

You will need

- Piece of plain muslin fabric
- Pencil
- Scissors
- Yellow thread and needle
- Small piece of tumbled citrine
- Dried sunflower seeds
- An item from your childhood that brought you joy
- Sun charm

Fold the piece of muslin in half and then draw a person outline so that you have two identical shapes. Don't make the outline too small, as it makes stuffing and sewing it more difficult. Cut the shapes out and keep the scraps. Start to sew the two dolls together, front and back, with simple stitches around the edges. When it's three-quarters of the way sewn together, place the citrine, sunflower seeds, childhood token, and scraps inside the doll. Sew the doll closed. Sew the Sun charm onto the center of the doll. If you're artistically minded, pull out your acrylic paints and paint some joyful symbols on the doll. In some cultures, it's recommended not to put a face on the doll, so if it doesn't feel right to do that, follow your intuition. You can work with this doll any time you're doing inner child work or have it on your altar. To really embrace your inner child while you're making this doll, put on your favorite childhood movie or music.

Crystal Magic Law

Citrine is like sunshine in a stone. It never requires cleansing, so it's perfect for use in poppets, magic pouches, and jars. A lot of citrine on the market is baked amethyst, which can be used, as natural citrine can be very expensive.

20
Judgement

Key concepts: Resurrection, awakening, evolution, discernment

The Judgement card represents the call from spirit to a higher purpose. This can manifest as a spiritual awakening, finding your own path in your career, or even a deeper understanding of your sacred relationships. This card offers you an invitation. You don't need to accept it, but things will never look the same again if you do. Judgement can also mean the literal definition of the word, from being overly judgmental of others and critical of your own self to showing level-headed discernment. It can also point to a legal judgment taking place. New life being given to an old project may also be connected to this card.

Outcome of Legal Matters Spread

The tarot spread for Judgement is perfect when you find yourself, or someone you love, in front of a judge or legal professional that has jurisdiction in the situation. This spread may help you prepare for your day in court. It can also show you the likely outcome of the matter. A tarot deck is not a suitable replacement for sound legal counsel, so make sure you do your mundane due diligence too.

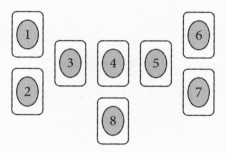

1. What is the essence of the legal dispute?
2. What do I know about the legal matter?
3. What am I unaware of about the legal matter?
4. What is my role/contribution in this situation?
5. What is the other party's role/contribution to the situation?
6. What do I need to prepare further?
7. Do I have the right legal representation?
8. What is the likely outcome of this matter?

Stop Caring What Other People Think Spell

Obsessing about what people think of you is a great way to suck the fun out of your life. And it's a waste of time. It can be hard to reprogram yourself to let go of people-pleasing, but it's empowering when you do so. The spell for Judgement is perfect for when you want to stop caring so much about what doesn't matter.

Best time to cast: **New Moon**

You will need

- A large orange
- Cutting board and sharp knife
- Candle carving tool or toothpick
- Orange candle
- Sandalwood essential oil
- Lighter or matches

Cut a small amount of the orange skin off the bottom of the orange so it will sit level. Cut the orange in half and place it in your workspace, where you'll burn the candle. Carve the words "I give no fucks" into the candle. Anoint the candle with some sandalwood oil and put the candle in the orange candleholder. Light the candle and say, "I give no fucks, no I don't care, I give no fucks, I'm beyond compare." Let the candle burn down, and watch your last fucks burn away.

Wood Magic Law

Sandalwood is a sacred wood that I highly recommend all magical workers have in their personal apothecary. It lends its power of confidence, calming, and consecration to all magical working.

21
The World

Key concepts: Achievement, completion, obtaining a goal, wholeness

The World arrives in a tarot reading when everything has come together perfectly and you've reached your desired outcome. It's the completion of one part of your life and the beginning of another. It's a fantastic card to have when you want to know if an undertaking is going to be successful or not, as this card points to yes. The World can also represent those times when you feel connected to your body and source, you recognize your place in the world, and you stand confidently in it. It's a sign to celebrate all you've accomplished before setting out for another new adventure.

Potential New Home Spread

The World tarot spread will let you know if the living space you're looking at is going to be right for you. It's one thing to fall in love with a house; it's quite another to find out it comes with unwanted guests or pesky neighbors. Before you sign anything, it's always important to do your due diligence, and this tarot spread can be part of that process. Bringing these findings to the realtor or property manager may save you money and the heartache of moving again because the place is not a good fit.

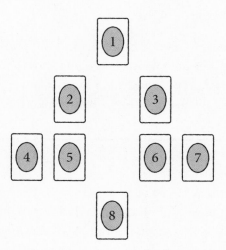

1. What kind of energy does this house have?

2. What secrets does this household have?

3. What does the realtor not want me to know?

4. What are the environmental considerations of this house?

5. What are the neighbors like?

6. Will I fit into the community?

7. Will I be safe and protected in this house?

8. What advice do the cards have for living in this space?

New House Blessing

We spend so much of our time in our living spaces, making them loving homes. House-warming parties and gifts have been a custom in many cultures for thousands of years. By setting your intentions and blessings in a new house, you're setting the space up for positivity. The World card is perfect for this spell, as we often live with loved ones who are much of what makes our world complete and magical.

Best time to cast: Anytime

You will need

- Pothos house plant
- Tumbled garnet stone
- Tumbled green jade stone

Place the tumbled stones in the soil of the plant. Hold your hands over the plant and speak this house blessing over it: "May you bless your home with protection to all who dwell within. Every day you grow, so will the power of your magic. Given with love, so mote it be!" Give the magical houseplant to the new owners the first time you visit them.

Plant Magic Law

Pothos plants are a perfect house blessing gift. It's a beginner-friendly plant that doesn't need a lot of attention. It'll survive in low light conditions and has magical protection, forgiveness, and resilience properties. It's poisonous if ingested by animals and children, so keep it in a place out of their reach.

Chapter 4
The Suit of Cups

The suit of Cups represents the deep waters of emotions, relationships, and intuition. This suit shows the wide range of the emotional aspects of our lives, reflecting the connections made with others, the feelings experienced about our circumstances, and our innermost desires and fears. When the suit of Cups is dominant in a reading, it signals that emotions are at the center of the situation. It may show a new relationship arriving soon, deepening feelings in a partnership, or resolving emotional conflicts. The Cups will ask you to look within and know how your emotions affect your life and decisions. This suit will ask you to reflect on the quality of your relationships and how you can heal any emotional wounds holding you back. The relationships you create and foster can open doors, lift you up, and enrich your life. They can also be stressful and difficult. The Cups are the tarot suit to work with whenever a situation is connected to the heart and the relationships with yourself and others.

Ace
of Cups

**Key concepts: New relationship, overflowing
emotions, love, feelings**

The Ace of Cups represents the divine offering of our emotions: the good, the bad, and the downright ugly. The Divine offers this overflowing vessel for us to take and experience life through our emotional selves. This is the beginning of our emotional understanding. It represents new emotions awakening and often means something new on the horizon that's going to have an emotional impact. New relationships—whether that's a new lover, a new friendship, and even news that someone you love is pregnant—are the Ace of Cups manifested.

Tap into Your Emotions Spread

The Ace of Cups represents the beginning of emotional exploration. Things are fresh and exciting, and there is a journey ahead for true fulfilment. Sometimes, it's hard to understand or even tap into our emotions, especially when they've been repressed, or we were told we're wrong by people in positions of power in our lives. The tarot spread for the Ace of Cups is a way for you to hold space for yourself and your emotions. Allow them some much-needed attention in a way that you can reflect on what you genuinely need to honor yourself.

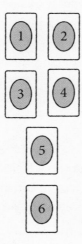

1. What emotion needs expressing?
2. What are my emotions trying to tell me?
3. What emotions do I need to release for my peace of mind?
4. What emotions am I experiencing that aren't mine?
5. How can I heal my emotional body?
6. How can I work on believing my emotions?

Tea of Peace Spell

Of course, the Ace of Cups spell must be a tea one! Tarot and tea are perfect partners. This magical tea can also be sipped while you carry out the tarot spread. Tea rituals have played an essential role throughout history in many cultures all over the world. It's a perfect way to embody the Ace of Cups and bring some peace to the waters in your body.

Best time to cast: **Anytime**

You will need

- A tea infuser or steeper
- One tablespoon of dried chamomile
- One tablespoon of dried lemon balm
- One tablespoon of dried rose petals
- A teacup
- Boiling water

Combine one tablespoon of each of the herbs in a tea pouch or infuser, and then hold the infuser in your hands. Close your eyes, breathe deeply, and connect to your heart chakra and sacral chakra, the place in your body where you store and feel emotion. When you feel that connection, say, "Magical plants of peace, thank you for your medicine, your magic and your healing." Place the infuser in your cup of freshly boiled water and allow it to steep for four to six minutes, then enjoy this cup of peace.

Magical Herb Law

Chamomile is an incredible and versatile flower and plant that aids in healing anxiety and insomnia. It is also an anti-inflammatory, and it boosts the immune system. That's just some of the properties of this magical herb!

2
of Cups

Key concepts: Unity, true love, compatibility, connection

Many readers often call the Two of Cups the "true love" tarot card, and I'm no exception. This is the card that represents a happy and harmonious relationship. The Two of Cups represents the early stages, but there is a strong possibility that the relationship will last beyond the initial attraction.

The two cups shown on the card are being offered and received. There is a true give and take, and the feelings are flowing both ways. Many symbols in the classic representations of the Two of Cups show that the relationship will also be one where healing can take place.

Where Is My True Love? Spread

So many people come to the tarot to find their true love, soulmates, twin flames, and even a hot summer fling, and why not? Love is something we need in life. Connection and care are vital to our well-being. The tarot spread for the Two of Cups can be used when you feel like you've tried almost everything to find a partner and have had no luck. It will help you be proactive in finding your ideal partner.

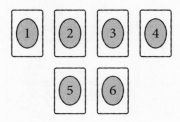

1. Where will I meet my true love?

2. What do I need to know about my true love?

3. What do I need to embrace on my journey to true love?

4. What do I need to stop doing in my search for true love?

5. What expectations do I need to drop about love?

6. Who is an ally for me to meet my true love?

Tarot Interpretation Tip

When seeking information about a location in a tarot card, think both literally and figuratively. If you pull Justice, for example, a law office, courtroom, legal section in a bookstore, or party where the host is a paralegal could all be possibilities!

Call In My True Love Spell

You'll become a love magnet with the tarot spell for the Two of Cups. This spell is best to cast at the New Moon under any astrological sign. As the power of the Moon increases, so will the power of this spell. Don't forget to go out and mingle after you've cast this spell so your new love can be drawn to you.

Best time to cast: New Moon

You will need

- One piece of paper
- A pink or red pen
- One lodestone or magnetic hematite
- A small lock or strands of your hair
- A pouch or envelope (white or red is the best color for this spell)

Write down what you truly desire in your true love on a piece of paper. Focus on what true love feels like to you. How do you want to be seen and loved? You can write down mundane things such as "Must have a stable job." While it is essential, don't forget to look at all sides of a relationship: the physical, emotional, mental, and spiritual. Be specific with what you desire.

Take the paper and read it over, ensuring you haven't left anything out. Chant the following as you complete the rest of the spell: "True love, true love come to me, my heart's desire, so mote it be!" Once you're happy with the list, place the loadstone and your hair in the pouch or envelope. Fold up the piece of paper and place it in the pouch/envelope as well. Close it and then hold it to your heart. Feel the love in your soul pouring out into the spell pouch, charging it with your loving energy and desire. The lodestone is now charged with your DNA and energy. If you want to give the spell an extra boost, hold the pouch to your heart chakra every day until the Full Moon and chant the line in the spell thirteen times. Store the pouch somewhere safe in your bedroom or on your altar.

3
of Cups

Key concepts: Friendship, indulgence, happiness, community

The Three of Cups holds the energy of good times, good people and good memories. There's nothing quite like spending time with the right people. People who share your interests and who will be there as you walk your journey in life. Whenever the Three of Cups comes up in a reading, it's time for a night out with friends! Social events are connected to this tarot card, so expect to get invitations in your inbox and ready your dancing shoes. Life is meant to be enjoyed; this card is an excellent reminder. Life will happen, no matter what worries or stresses you have. Don't let it pass you by and sit on the sidelines.

Friendship Spread

Making friends as an adult can be difficult. People tend to stick with a group of people they've known for a long time who are in comfortable routines. Finding a social hobby is one of the best pieces of advice I can pass on to you. It worked for me when I moved to a different country and will work for you. Whether you like tabletop games, hiking, quilting, lifting weights, or wine tasting, groups of people out there would love to have you join them. The Friendship tarot spread for the Three of Cups is an overall friendship spread, exploring the different aspects of being a friend.

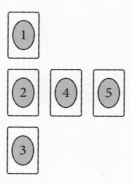

1. What gift do I bring to friendships?

2. What do I need to heal around trusting people?

3. What can I do to support my friends more?

4. What can I do to be my own best friend?

5. What advice does the Three of Cups have for me around friendship?

Find a New BFF Spell

The tarot spell for this card will help you find a new friend or even a new best friend. Perhaps you've been burned in the past or had less than positive experiences with the people you've endeavored to foster friendships with. Making friendship bracelets was something I remember doing when I was younger, and the magic you can weave into them is so powerful. This spell will aid you in being open to friends and finding the right people to celebrate life with.

Best time to cast: New Moon

You will need

- Embroidery floss in the colors blue, pink, and green
- Scissors
- Tape or safety pin to secure strands down

Cut four strands of embroidery floss to a length of sixteen inches. Tie a knot a couple of inches down the threads. You'll need that extra couple of inches at the top to complete the bracelet. Take one of the colored threads and create a shape that looks like a number four; this is done by laying the thread across the other four from left to right. You then pull that thread through the loop. The thread will go under the four others and through the loop. Make sure you pull the thread to a tight knot. Do this for a time and then pick the next color, laying the one you were working on down with the other four and keep repeating the process until you have sections of the bracelet in each color. This is known as the square knot.

Art Magic Tip

When creating knots, it's beneficial to be able to see how it's done in real-time. Find a YouTube video of a Chinese ladder friendship bracelet tutorial so you can see the knots being made. That way, you can focus on the energy and desire you're putting into the spell, not the knots.

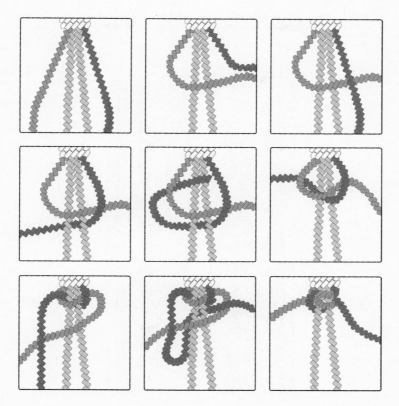

While you're doing this, hold the space of friendship in your energy. You can repeat the following affirmation as you knot your spell into a bracelet: "I deserve and accept positive friendships into my life with ease and grace, so mote it be."

Finish the bracelet off by tying it to your wrist or ankle. As you wear this bracelet, you carry the spell with you, and it will bring the right people to you as you go out and experience that social hobby and meet new folks.

4
of Cups

Key concepts: Apathy, boredom, fatigue, disconnection

The Four of Cups represents the energy of apathy on many levels. Usually, the figure in the card has closed-off body language. There is no movement, either. Everything is stagnant; water that doesn't move is a breeding ground for nasty things. Anyone who's tried to re-engage in life after a long illness or a difficult time knows that getting your energy moving is the hardest part. Everything is right in front of you when this card is presented. You just have to be willing to take what's being offered to you and do something with it.

Release Apathy Spread

When you find yourself stuck in a position where you're feeling bored, disillusioned, and uninterested in life, pull out a tarot deck in your collection that brings you joy and allow those Four of Cups feelings some space to be explored. Give yourself the gift of perspective, and maybe even a little kick in the pants from the universe, to help release the grip that they've had on you. This tarot spread is not a replacement for taking care of your mental health, and if any of the Four of Cups feelings remain too long, please get some professional assistance.

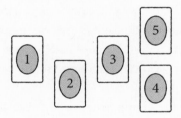

1. What thoughts are keeping me unmotivated?

2. What needs of mine aren't being met?

3. What are my feelings trying to tell me?

4. What positive options in front of me are being ignored?

5. What steps can I take to release my stagnation?

Reengage Joy Spell

Joy is a surefire panacea when you're suffering from stagnation in your life. This spell is designed to bring pleasure into your life by lifting your energy to meet the joyful opportunities around you. Celebrating your wins, no matter how small, is also essential during times of weariness. Applaud your efforts and share them with a friend. It does wonders for keeping the positive energies flowing.

Best time to cast: Anytime

You will need

- A yellow item
- A symmetrical item
- A vessel that can hold water
- Something that reminds you of a happy memory
- A thing that you find beautiful
- Something that makes you smile

This spell is a journey spell. You'll be exploring the world to find joy. This spell is even better if you can do it with someone you love. Pick a location in your area that you'd like to explore. This spell is a good reason for a road trip. Some suggestions are a local park, thrift store, marketplace, art gallery, or museum. The wonderful thing about art galleries and museums is that they're usually free and brimming with work that can spark joy.

As you explore these areas, find the things listed above. Take photos of them if you can, or if you're out in nature, you can even bring home some of these things to put on your altar.

When you return home after your journey of joy, place the photos in your journal as a reminder of the happiness you can find all around you.

5
of Cups

Key concepts: Grief, loss, despair, regret

The Five of Cups is never easy to receive in a reading. No matter the nature of the loss that accompanies this card, it's something that we all experience at some point in our lives. We wouldn't be able to experience happiness and love without the bitterness of sadness and loss. Some of the key symbols often seen in the card hold the keys to help this energy move to a more positive place. Not all of the cups are tipped over; there is a bridge over the water, a way back to your community in the distance. The Five of Cups is also a reminder that sometimes tricky feelings or memories come out of nowhere. Healing from loss isn't a one-and-done situation. Some days, you're able to lift your head and see the Sun, and other days, you have to hold space for your more complex feelings.

Feel to Heal Spread

The risk of the Five of Cups is when we get lost in our sorrow and can't move on. There are many reasons that someone may get stuck in grief and despair. Our emotions are a complex realm, and there is no one-size-fits-all solution for loss. The tarot spread for the Five of Cups is built around one of my favorite sayings about unpleasant feelings: you have to feel and deal to heal. Don't bury your emotions and true feelings; it'll only prolong the experience of pain. So when you feel those hard feelings, use this tarot spread to support your healing journey through them.

1. What does my grieving self need?
2. How can I embrace my feelings more?
3. How can I acknowledge my pain in a healthy way?
4. What is holding me back from accepting aid?
5. How can I best support my healing journey?

Safe Place to Grieve Spell

This tarot spell will create a safe place for you to grieve. Most people have many responsibilities and limited time and energy they can allocate for their own healing, so this is a gift you can give yourself when you need it. While the space you're going to create is small, it's incredibly impactful.

Best time to cast: Full Moon to Waning Moon

You will need

- A glass jar with a lid (mason jars are a perfect size)
- Enough water that will fill the jar three-quarters of the way
- A tablespoon of dandelion flowers and leaves
- Small pieces of paper
- Blue pen

Take your jar of water and place it somewhere where the light of the Full Moon can bathe it in its light. Even if the night sky is cloudy, the magic will still work. You can do the rest of the spell the following morning.

Gather your jar and the spell ingredients and sit somewhere that has a window. Place the dandelions in the water. Bring your focus to your breath and breathe in deeply and fully while feeling the energy of your heart chakra. Rub the palm of your left hand over your heart and allow your grief to come to the surface. Write down some keywords or concepts of that grief on one of the pieces of paper with the blue pen. If you find that you have tears in this process, you can collect them and place them in the jar, too. When you're ready to put the paper in the jar, do so. Spend as much time as you need with any other feelings or memories that come up, write them down, and place them in the jar. When you're ready to close out the spell, put the lid on the jar and place it in the same place where the moonlight can do its work. When the Moon wanes to dark, take the jar of water and water a plant in your garden with it.

Magical Flower Law

Dandelion: This sunny flower is magically associated with acknowledging and releasing grief as well as blowing the seeds in the wind to make a wish.

6
of Cups

Key concepts: Memories, childhood, reunion, past influences

This tarot card brings with it the energy of the past. For some, it's a welcome nostalgia for the things that brought us joy growing up. For others, it brings painful memories. It's often seen as a positive card that reminds us of times when the world was large beyond our comprehension, and anything was possible. This card connects us to children; whether it's our inner child or our own children, there is always something to learn from the child archetype. Bring a sense of wonder and innocence to your situation and see what you'll discover.

Past Life Spread

Our past lives are not something that chains us in this lifetime but are opportunities to learn about different aspects of ourselves. There is an idea that we're bound to keep learning lessons throughout our incarnations until it's fully integrated into our souls. Whether you've met someone with whom you've felt a connection you can't explain or are having recurring dreams of a life you've lived before, the Past Life tarot spread, created for the Six of Cups, is a way you can explore your past lives.

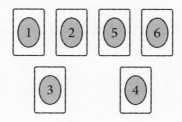

1. What kind of person was I in this past life?
2. What role did I play in this past life?
3. What did I bring into this life from my past life?
4. What is the relevance of this past life to my current situation?
5. How can I heal the connection to this life?
6. What lesson am I still learning?

Release Past Chains Spell

The Six of Cups spell is a multipurpose spell that can be used when you have a memory or past situation that needs to be removed from your life. Our past is something we can't run away from; it makes you who you are, but don't get too lost in the past and forget to be present. So when you find you're telling the same stories about your past or unable to let go, use this spell and give yourself the gift of emotional freedom.

Best time to cast: Waning Moon

You will need

- Small picture of a Six of Cups tarot card
- A pen
- Six four-inch lengths of twine
- Scissors

On the Six of Cups card copy, write down the past situation from which you want to be released. Create a chain of loops with the twine lengths you have and as you complete the chain loop, think about the situation you wrote about on the card. Pour as much energy as you can into those pieces of twine. Read what you've written on the Six of Cups card out loud as you hold your chain. Think about why you're ready to let it go and build your resolve. When you're ready, take your pair of scissors and cut each of the links. As you cut each twine chain link, say, "I release the hold the past has on me, I am free, so mote it be." Cut up the picture of the Six of Cups as well. Take the clippings and throw them away or bury them away from your property.

Tarot Magic Tip

Using a tarot card in a spell is a beautiful way to bring complex energy like memories to a spell. I use photocopies of the card for spells as I wouldn't dream of cutting or marking up one of my tarot decks. Please also use natural fiber twine so that it can compost when you bury it.

7
of Cups

Key concepts: Fantasy, wishful thinking, options, choice

Anyone who's been faced with a choice with many tempting options has embodied the energy of the Seven of Cups. Each cup shows you a desire or an opportunity. The fact that they're all high in the sky indicates that these are choices dreamed up via our emotional ties and fantasies. It's essential to consider each option carefully, as action needs to follow once a choice has been made. The Seven of Cups also represents procrastination and being overwhelmed with the choices in front of you.

Is This Real? Spread

The tarot spread for this the Seven of Cups is best to use when you're unsure whether your feelings are real. Wanting to know whether the person you're interested in is just saying all the right things but won't be there when it matters is another way you can use this tarot spread. The Cups represent the realm of emotion, with each cup representing a potential reality. Choices around the heart often feel like the hardest to make. It's during these times when you want to use this tarot spread.

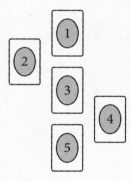

1. How do they really feel?
2. What do they really want?
3. What are their intentions with me?
4. Is this connection worth pursuing?
5. What do my guides want me to know about this person?

Sweet Fantasy Bath Spell

The spell for the Seven of Cups is to be cast when you feel ready to bring a fantasy to life. All that daydreaming is about to become reality. Water is a wonderful conduit for dreams, desires, and fantasies. Ritual baths allow you to be wrapped in magical water. Afterward, you'll glow with the energy you want to manifest. If you don't have a bath, you can use the magical bath pouch as a skin exfoliator in the shower.

Best time to cast: New to Full Moon

You will need

- Epsom salts
- Glass jar
- Dried rose petals or essential oil
- Dried lavender flowers or essential oil
- Dried calendula flowers or essential oils
- Sweet orange essential oil
- Spoon
- Muslin drawstring pouch or tea cloth pouch

Place your Epsom salts in the glass jar. Add in the dried flowers or oils to your personal preference. Always start with a small amount and then slowly add more if you feel it needs it. A little goes a long way. Add a few drops of the sweet orange essential oil. Mix it all with the spoon. As you mix, chant the following seven times: "Dreams to reality, I call it to be, manifest before me, so mote it be." Once it's well mixed, place the lid on the jar. Allow the salts to sit for at least a few hours. Use the spoon to fill the cloth pouch with some of the mixture and place it in your bath the next time you bathe. Allow the magical qualities of the oils and flowers to bathe you in manifesting energies.

8
of Cups

Key concepts: Walking away, moving on,
abandonment, withdrawal

The Eight of Cups comes up whenever there is a need for a new direction in life. You may have had a change of heart or a change of circumstances that makes everything need a reset. Knowing what you're worth and going on a journey of self-discovery is also connected to this card. Leaving is not always a sign of weakness. Doing what is necessary often takes a lot of courage.

Should I Stay or Should I Go? Spread

The tarot spread for the Eight of Cups is one that I've used with my clients and personally on a number of occasions. When you've invested a lot of time, energy, and resources into a relationship, it can be tough to walk away, whether professional or personal. This spread will give you perspective outside of your own fears and allow you to make an empowered and informed plan for your future.

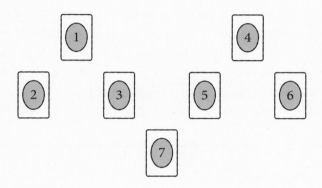

1. What will happen if I stay?

2. What will I lose if I stay?

3. What will I gain if I stay?

4. What will happen if I go?

5. What will I lose if I go?

6. What will I gain if I go?

7. What advice is there for my future?

Let It Go Spell

Walking away is not always easy. So when you need a good kick in the pants to do what's best for you, use the Eight of Cups spell. Being mentally ready to release something doesn't always mean that you're emotionally prepared to let go. This spell brings your emotional body in alignment with your choices.

Best time to cast: Waning Moon

You will need

- Eight river stones
- Sharpie or a black painting pen

Write what you want to release on each of the river stones. It could be fear of being alone, fear of change, or other people's opinions, whatever comes up for you in this situation. Take the stones to a natural place with moving water, such as a lake, creek, or ocean. As you stand near the water's edge, read the stone and throw it in to the water as hard as you can. Repeat this process with each stone to let it all go. Ensure you're doing this spell safely by ensuring that others are not in your line of fire as you throw stones. Sing your favorite song about letting things go for an extra boost of power. If you can't access a natural body of water, leave the stones out when it rains and allow the rain to help you let it go.

Elemental Magic Tip

Any body of water is a powerful conduit for spells connected to your emotions. Flowing and moving water is terrific for spells requiring a change of your emotional state and healing.

9
of Cups

Key concepts: Self-esteem, joy, fulfilment,
contentment, optimism

The Nine of Cups brings with it the energy of happiness and feeling good about yourself. You're more likely to make decisions that will create joy and favorable circumstances in all areas of your life if you have healthy self-esteem.

When you feel good, you shine from the inside out, making manifesting your ideal life so much easier and more fun. This card brings its positive influence into a reading.

Self-Love Spread

One of the best ways to bring the Nine of Cups energy into your life is through self-love practices. Self-love behaviors have proven to re-enforce healthy choices and improve mental health and motivation. The tarot spread for the Nine of Cups can help you revamp your self-love routine and bring a boost to your self-esteem.

1. How can I be kinder to myself this week?
2. What self-love action do I need to take this week?
3. Where can I be more patient with myself?
4. What does my heart need from me?
5. How can I embody joy more?

Love and Accept Me Spell

Self-acceptance is a vital part of loving yourself. No one is perfect, no matter what filters they use on social media. Accepting yourself, flaws and all, not only is a positive step for yourself but can also help you understand and love others with more compassion and kindness. This is a spell you can use at any time whenever you're feeling a little down on yourself.

Best time to cast: **Anytime**

You will need
- A tumbled rose quartz crystal
- Rose essential oil
- A crystal cage necklace

Take your rose quartz and anoint it with a couple of drops of the rose essential oil. As you do so, say, "I love and accept myself, flaws and all. Every day, every way, love, I do call." Place the stone in the cage necklace, wear it throughout the day, and allow love to come to you with ease.

Crystal Magic Law

Rose quartz is one of the most versatile love crystals the mineral kingdom has gifted us. Its gentle energy opens and soothes the hearts of all who work with it.

10
of Cups

Key concepts: Family, reunions, peace, commitment

The Ten of Cups shows an idyllic scene of a happy family under the blessing of a rainbow of full cups. Everything about the card is open and welcoming. This card points to relationships that are likely to go the distance and be worthwhile for your time and commitment. Whenever the Ten of

Cups comes up in a reading, positive times are ahead, especially when you spend time with the people you love.

Happy Home Spread

If your home feels more like a battleground than a sanctuary, the tarot spread for the Ten of Cups can be valuable for reflection and positive change. Living with others always comes with challenges. People are complex, and life is stressful at times. While you can only be responsible for your actions and energy, a tarot reading can help you be more empowered with the boundaries you set in your home.

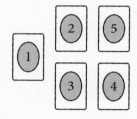

1. What is blocking the family's connection?
2. What needs to be communicated more clearly?
3. How can I promote safe energy in the home?
4. What energy needs to be welcomed into the home?
5. What protection does my family need?

Home Harmony Spell Jar

The Home Harmony Spell Jar is an easy and effective spell jar that brings positive energy to the home and all who dwell there. Creating the spell jar on a Full Moon or New Moon is the most effective time of the Moon's cycle for this type of magic.

Best time to cast: Full Moon or New Moon

You will need

- Blue pen
- Piece of paper
- Small glass jar with a lid
- Sugar cubes
- Honey
- Lavender (dried or a few drops of essential oil)

Take your pen and piece of paper and write down your home's address and this blessing for a happy home: "Lavender flower and honey of earth, cleanse and bless this home and hearth. Drive away all harm and fear; only love may enter here!" Fold the piece of paper up and place it in the jar. Put a sugar cube or two, the honey, and the lavender flowers in the jar. Seal the jar and place it somewhere safe in your home. Replace this spell jar every season to renew the blessing.

Page
of Cups

Key concepts: Empathy, kindness, sensitivity, imagination

The Page of Cups communicates emotions both evident and hidden. They often represent a person with innocent energy or a younger person. This card in readings often comes up when a new baby is announced.

Empathic Powers Spread

Being an empath is a gift unless you aren't able to set boundaries and fine-tune your skills. Without adequate protections and boundaries, you're more susceptible to taking on other people's pain and energy as your own. The Page of Cups tarot spread will allow you to tap in to your empathic powers and identify potential blind spots.

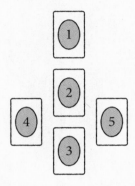

1. What boundaries do I need to put in place?
2. What energies do I need to release?
3. How can I heal my own empathic wounds?
4. How can I best develop my empathic powers right now?
5. How can I use my empathic powers in my life?

Empath Protection Aura Spray

The spell for the Page of Cups is one of my all-time favorite magical tools. I use it daily in my practice. Aura sprays are easy to use once they've been created, and you can take them with you anywhere.

Best time to cast: Anytime

You will need

- One two-ounce amber glass or aluminum spray bottle
- Sage essential oil
- Cedarwood essential oil

- Rosemary essential oil
- One small smokey quartz crystal
- Enough spring or moonwater to fill the bottle

Put thirteen drops of sage oil, seven drops of cedarwood oil, and seven drops of rosemary oil in your spray bottle. Place the small smokey quartz crystal in the bottle. Fill the bottle with the water and secure the spray top in place. Give the bottle a good shake and say, "Envelop me in protective warmth; bring shielding from the east, west, south, and north." You can use this spray whenever you need. Ensure you shake it well before use. You can also recite the charm each time you use it for an extra energy boost.

Knight of Cups

Key concepts: Romance, your heart's desire, creative endeavors, new lover

The Knight of Cups calls for us to act on behalf of our hearts and emotions, from asking your crush out on a date to writing that poem that's been inside your heart for months. Following your heart can be a little scary, but the Knight of Cups knows that "What if?" is harder to live with than taking the risk. Romantic news and communication, or possibly a new lover, often follows the arrival of the Knight of Cups. The Knight's energy isn't one of serious commitment, so have fun and don't overthink things.

Hot Lover or a Dud? Spread

The tarot spread for the Knight of Cups evokes the not-so-serious fun of the card. There's nothing wrong with wanting to know if someone is worth your time. Everyone has their own idea of what makes someone a hot lover, so hold the intention of what that means for you when you use this tarot spread. Having a person in mind is best when you do this tarot spread. Of course, you don't have to use this spread if you don't like conducting third-party readings.

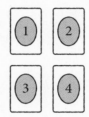

1. Is this person safe to be intimate with?

2. Are we a match physically?

3. Will we have good chemistry as lovers?

4. Can this person give me what I want at this time?

Call In a New Lover Spell

The Knight of Cups spell is one of my favorites and one that I've used in my own magical work in the past. The intention of this spell is to bring someone into your life for a passionate love affair. This person is here for a good time, not a long one, so it is best not to cast this if you're looking for long-term love.

Best time to cast: **New Moon**

You will need

- Pink pen
- Image of the Knight of Cups
- Pink candle with holder
- Toothpick
- Rose essential oil
- Lighter

Take some time to think about what you desire in a new lover. Hold that feeling in your energy, take the pink pen, and write what you desire on the back of the image of the Knight of Cups. Be specific with the details, but don't target any one person. For example, you may put—A masculine person, between twenty-five to thirty-five years of age, great kisser, loves to cuddle, in my city. You can add more details; this is just an example of where to start. Take your toothpick and write your name and date of birth on the candle. Anoint the candle with a couple of drops of rose oil while reading your lover list on the Knight of Cups. Place the candle and holder on top of the image and light the candle. Close your eyes and chant twelve times: "Come to me, lover; come to me, love; come to me, lover, matching my Knight of Cups hereof." Allow the candle to burn down in a safe place.

Queen
of Cups

Key concepts: Compassion, giving, nurturing, tenderness

The Queen of Cups is emotional nurturing personified. They bring with them compassion and understanding of deep feelings. She's a vessel of empathy and intuition, often drawn to esoteric topics. The Queen of Cups knows how to speak about matters of the heart and understands how important emotional health is. This Queen is the person you want to talk to during emotional turmoil or a bad breakup.

Self-Compassion Spread

One of the Queen of Cups tendencies is to hold how you're feeling inside because you're busy taking care of everyone else. Bottling up emotions always has consequences, and they are rarely healthy or enjoyable. The spread created for this tarot card is an invitation to turn your nurturing gifts onto yourself. You experience your emotional body in your hormones, nervous systems, and the relationship your body has with water and touch.

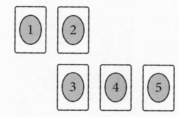

1. How can I nurture myself today?
2. What self-judgments need to be released right now?
3. What action can I take to embrace positive feelings?
4. What misunderstood feelings need compassion now?
5. What emotions need support right now?

Third Eye Psychic Balm

The Queen of Cups is in tune with their intuition in a profound way. They're often connected at all times to their inner knowing. This psychic balm will enhance your tarot readings and magical workings. You can anoint your wrists, your temples, and even your third eye. Do a spot test on your skin before placing it all over yourself to ensure you won't have an allergic reaction to any ingredients. When working with this psychic balm, you're embodying the Queen of Cups.

Best time to cast: Full Moon

You will need

- A stovetop
- Double boiler
- Mixing spoon
- Two tablespoons of beeswax beads
- Three-quarters of a cup of jojoba or sweet almond oil
- Three drops of mugwort essential oil
- Two drops of eucalyptus essential oil
- Two drops of bay essential oil
- Two drops of yerba santa essential oil
- Clean container with lid
- Label and pen

In the top section of the double boiler, add the beeswax. Slowly add the jojoba or sweet almond oil when it's melted down halfway. You don't want any of these ingredients to get too hot, so creating this slow and steady is the best way to do it. Allow the oil and beeswax to combine together completely.

Take the bowl off the heat and add the essential oil drops. Mix these in well. Smell the mixture to make sure it's pleasant to you. You can adjust the oils to make sure you like the aroma of the balm. You won't want to work with it if you don't like the smell. Next, pour the mixture into your clean container. Leave the lid off and allow it to set. Write the name of the balm on the label and the date you prepared it, and place it on the container when the balm has completely set. Use as needed. Store it with the lid securely tightened in a cool place.

King of Cups

Key concepts: Maturity, emotional intelligence, diplomatic, deep

The King of Cups knows their emotions well because they've dared to walk the path of shadow integration. Once started, this is often a life-long journey. They're a person who is able to have deep conversations and be diplomatic in the process. They care deeply about the people they love and are devoted to the people they choose to take care of. People trust someone who holds the King of Cups' energy because they take responsibility for their emotions.

Shadow Work Spread

The King of Cups tarot spread is a great place to start with your shadow work. Shadow work is when you intentionally work with your subconscious self to bring the parts of yourself that are hidden into the light of understanding and integration. This often includes personality traits that you dislike or that trigger an adverse reaction or emotion. As shadow work tends to be intense, the spread is a smaller offering for you to start with.

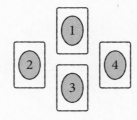

1. What is the shadow aspect I'm ignoring?
2. Why have I been suppressing this?
3. What is it trying to show me?
4. What healing step do I take now?

Shadow Integration Incense Blend

The spell for the King of Cups is an incense blend you can burn whenever you're doing shadow work. This can be for yourself or for others. It's a perfect way to create an integration vibration during tarot readings, meditations and even self-love work, as it is also shadow work. This blend can pack a punch, so you'll only need a little amount when you burn it on a charcoal disk.

Best time to cast: Full Moon or Waning Moon

You will need

- Mortar and pestle
- One tablespoon of cedar powder or chips
- Half a tablespoon of frankincense resin
- One tablespoon of dried lavender flowers
- One tablespoon of dried black cohosh root or powder
- Three drops of patchouli essential oil
- Spoon
- Glass jar with lid

Add the dried materials to a mortar and pestle and combine them well. Once they are blended well together, add three drops of patchouli essential oil and mix that in. Spoon the incense blend into the glass jar and use it when you need it. Store in a cool place out of direct sunlight.

Chapter 5
The Suit of Wands

The suit of Wands is associated with creativity, ambition, careers, and action. This fiery suit brings energy and enthusiasm to a reading, highlighting aspects of our lives that involve personal growth, initiative, and enterprise. Wands represent the driving force behind our passions and pursuits, often signaling a time of decision-making and new ventures. When Wands cards are the dominant suit in a reading, they suggest actions that must be taken and highlight areas in life requiring immediate attention. The Wands want you to actively engage with the world. Put your ideas and creativity into motion and be a cocreator with the universe. The Wands suit can show you what is driving your actions in life and help you maintain your motivation while working on large projects. Tarot readings and spells that connect to work and career are well suited for the Wands cards as they can guide you toward fulfilling and fruitful endeavors.

Ace
of Wands

Key concepts: Ambition, a spark, passion, vitality

The Ace of Wands is a calling from spirit to take the wand and run with it. New beginnings around career, creative endeavors, and physical energy are all territory of this card. If you've been waiting for an opportunity to share your gifts and talents with the world, you'll want to embrace the Ace of Wands' energy. Its arrival is also a sign of new projects coming your way. The potential is there; now it's up to you to do something with it.

Find Your Passion Spread

If you've been unable to find your passion in life or are in a slump, then the spread for the Ace of Wands is an excellent partner to invigorate your energy. Whether you're worried about trying and failing or being perfect, you can use the tarot to get out of your own way and move forward.

1. What is holding me back?
2. Where should I be looking for my passion?
3. What action can I take to release my potential?
4. What can help me feel more passionate?

Ignite Your Inner Spark Spell

If you've ever said you need someone to metaphorically light a fire under your butt to get you moving, the spell for the Ace of Wands is designed for you. It's also just a super fun spell. The Wands suit can literally represent a magical wand, and the sparklers you use in this spell perfectly embody this card's energy.

Best time to cast: Full Moon

You will need

- A pack of sparklers
- A lighter or match

This spell needs to be done outside or in a well-ventilated area. Under the light of the Full Moon, take one of your sparklers and a lighter, and while saying the following, ignite the sparkler: "I want to spark, I want to shine, I call upon my light divine, see this flicker in the dark, seek me out, my inner flame lit, I proclaim, like a lark." Joyfully wave the sparkler around, writing your name in the air. Envision this as the beacon for rekindling your inner power and fire.

2
of Wands

Key concepts: Choice, direction, waiting, hesitation

There is a sense of safety in the Two of Wands. When you don't decide or act on your projects and desires, you risk nothing. The issue is that you gain nothing by sitting on the sidelines of your own life. While there is power in planning and anticipation, getting stuck is rarely people's goal. This card has a sense of hope, like anything is possible, and the journey is still new and exciting.

Is This Partnership a Good Idea? Spread

Being unsure of a business or creative partnership is an aspect of the Two of Wands. You know what you want and are almost ready to take the plunge, but something is holding you back. The tarot spread for this card can provide some perspective so you can see what may or may not work within the collaboration. While using the wisdom of the tarot to help you make a decision, remember to honor your intuition when it comes to the people you work with.

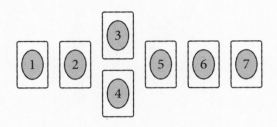

1. What can I expect from this partnership?
2. Are there any areas of concern within this partnership?
3. Will this partnership yield positive outcomes?
4. Will we be able to navigate the road bumps during this partnership?
5. What area of this partnership should I lean into?
6. What area of this partnership should I delegate?
7. Is there some final advice to consider about the future of this partnership?

Find the Perfect Work Partner Spell

This tarot spell has been created for the times when you have a fantastic idea or project you want to undertake and want an amazing person to collaborate with. We all have strengths and areas where we shine, and finding partners who complement or shore up our weaknesses can ensure success.

Best time to cast: New Moon

You will need

- A small figurine (Lego mini or something similar is perfect)
- A small box (ensure all of the spell contents will fit in this box)
- Dried lavender flowers
- One bay leaf
- A gold or copper coin

Hold the miniature figure in your hands and close your eyes. Envision, with as much detail as possible, what you need and want in a work partner. See yourself working with them successfully. Don't target anyone specifically with this visualization. Feel the productivity and success you'll have together. When you're ready, place the doll in the box with the lavender, bay leaf, and coin. Close the lid and say, "I'm ready to work, I'm here to succeed, come and be the work partner I need. Lavender brings peace, protection from the bay, and many coins we'll make every day. You will arrive when the Moon peaks in power, and our projects will bloom like a heavenly flower. So mote it be!" Place the box in your workspace so it won't get disturbed and allow the right person to present themselves to you soon.

3
of Wands

Key concepts: Foresight, travel, future planning, progress

The Three of Wands asks that we consider our actions, long-term goals, and duties, and not just short-term gratification. Your hard work will pay off. Remember to keep your goals in mind when carrying out your tasks. Another critical aspect of the card is that of motivation and sharing your vision and gifts with the world. There is no space or time to play small. It's a sign to move forward with confidence and trust in your abilities and skills.

Long-Term Goal Spread

The tarot spread for the Three of Wands will tell you whether a long-term goal has potential. As this is the card of foresight, being able to judge whether you want to commit to something long-term can help your confidence levels going in. It can also help you stay motivated when the less glamorous aspects of your work kick in.

Tarot Interpretation Tip

When interpreting a tarot card for positive or negative outcomes, trust your first intuitive hit when you flip the card over. Even better, assign a yes, no, or maybe to each of the cards and have that list in an easy-to-access place for reference.

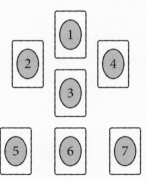

1. Will I find success with the goal I have in mind?

2. What may block my success?

3. What support will I need to achieve my goal?

4. What do I need to prioritize in the next three months?

5. What do I need to prioritize in the next six months?

6. What do I need to prioritize in the next nine months?

7. What do I need to prioritize in the next twelve months?

Reach My Goals Spell

Nothing feels better than reaching a goal you set out to achieve; however, running out of motivation and drive befalls everyone. The spell for the Three of Wands is a spell that you work with from the New Moon to the Full Moon. As the energy of the spell increases, so will the momentum in your work. It's like taking a daily shot of motivation but in spell form.

Best time to cast: New Moon to Full Moon

You will need

- Orange pen
- A piece of orange paper
- A piece of red jasper

On the day of the New Moon, take the orange pen and the orange piece of paper and write down the goal you want to achieve. Fold this three times and place it somewhere that's connected to your goal. For example, it could be in your wallet if it's a financial goal or tucked in a book if you're working on writing something; anywhere that correlates between the spell and your goal. Hold the red jasper in your hands daily and say, "I've got this, I've got this, I've got this. One step at a time, success will be mine. I've got this, I've got this, I've got this." Place the jasper piece on your altar or by your workspace when you're finished chanting.

Crystal Magic Law

Does size matter? Many spells call for crystals to be used. They're wonderful correspondences for magic. You don't need large stones for spellwork. Most often, a small tumbled stone will do the trick. You can use larger pieces, of course; however, once you've programmed the stone for a specific part of magical work, you'll need to cleanse it before you can use it again.

4
of Wands

Key concepts: Security, celebration, community, success

The Four of Wands is a card of celebration and gatherings that bring people together. There is a sense of excitement that comes with this card. A sense of belonging connects people when this card comes up. Each one of the wands can be seen as representing the elements that make a good party happen: the people, the place, the vibe, and the reason. Weddings, engagements, birthdays, and housewarming parties are all events are connected to this card.

Birthday Spread

Birthdays are always worth celebrating, if not for the cake alone. Whether you love the attention of a large party or want to share your birthday with an intimate group of friends quietly, this tarot spread is a beautiful way to honor your day. Don't forget that making a wish and blowing out your birthday candles is a form of magic, so make the most of your birthday when it comes to your magic, too!

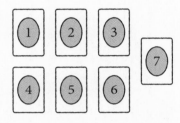

1. What should I celebrate today in addition to my birthday?
2. What was the primary lesson of my previous year?
3. What is the energetic theme of the year to come?
4. What are the energies around my relationships in the coming year?
5. What are the energies around my work and career over the course of the year?
6. What are my health and well-being energies this coming year?
7. What are the energies and spiritual lessons I will encounter this year?

Newlywed Blessing

Since weddings and marriage ceremonies often accompany the Four of Wands in readings, the spell for this card is a blessing for anyone who is getting married. A flashy wedding doesn't mean a marriage will be easy, and the wedding day itself, big or small, is just the beginning of married life. This blessing can be given to any couple who's walking down the aisle or going to review their vows.

Best time to cast: Cast any time before the couple's wedding

You will need

- A plate
- Salt
- Three tablespoons of dried rose petals
- One tablespoon of dried rosemary
- One tablespoon of dried vervain
- A horseshoe
- A pink Sharpie or paint pen

Most of us don't have easy access to horseshoes, but you can find them online or by reaching out to a stable to buy them used. Just make sure the horseshoe is clean and sanitized before you use it in the spell. You could also use ornamental horseshoes for this spell.

Mix the salt, dried herbs, and flowers together and place them on the plate. Take the pink Sharpie or paint pen and write the full names of the people getting married and the date of the ceremony on the horseshoe. Place the horseshoe on top of the salt mix. Leave it overnight. This purifies the horseshoe and adds magical properties to the shoe. Give the horseshoe to the couple on their wedding day. It's even better if they can place it on the table where they have their first meal together as a married couple. The horseshoe will need to be taken to the couple's home and secured to a wall. It's essential that its secured upright to remain a symbol of good luck for their marriage and for their home. Bag the salt mix and give that to the couple as well. They can use it as protective salt for their home.

Herbal Magic Law

Vervain's magical properties include blessing, purification, and protection. It's a versatile magical herb that can be used in many spells.

5
of Wands

Key concepts: Competition, conflict, struggle, opposition

There is a sense of chaos in the Five of Wands. There is no plan and every-one involved thinks they know best. Some people thrive in this kind of environment. They love being pushed to see what they're made of. Other people find it too overwhelming and stand to the side and let everyone fight over the next best move. While this card can feel negative, not all challenges are sent to break you. Sometimes they are the wake-up call you need so you don't get complacent.

Take On This Challenge Spread

Use this tarot spread to empower your choices and actions when faced with a challenge that you want to tackle. Knowing how to equip yourself and what to avoid can make all the difference in having a positive outcome. I believe we're never given a challenge we can't overcome, but it doesn't mean it must be a horrible experience. While you carry out the tarot reading, hold the challenge you're facing in your energy. Think about it as clearly as you can while you shuffle the cards so the energy of the challenge is represented in the cards you draw.

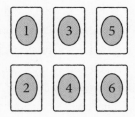

1. Why has this challenge come my way?
2. What will I get out of this challenge?
3. What is the main obstacle to overcoming this challenge?
4. What strategy is best to lean into for this challenge?
5. What is the first step to overcome this challenge?
6. What is the final blessing of this challenge?

Have Courage Bracelet Spell

People give themselves courage in many ways, from a few shots of liquor to a pep talk from a friend. The Five of Wands spell is like a magical shot of courage in crystal form, and you won't get a hangover. All of the suggested gemstone beads will bring supportive energy to your root and sacral chakras. These gemstones are associated with courage and

158 ✳ CHAPTER 5

facing our fears. If you ever feel like the gemstones need a magical boost, leave the bracelet under the light of the Full Moon for a night. These bracelets also make wonderful magical gifts.

Best time to cast: Full Moon

You will need

- Carnelian gemstone beads
- Red jasper gemstone beads
- Smoky quartz gemstone beads
- Scissors
- Elastic bracelet cord

If you can get only one of these gemstone bead types, use what you can. You'll need enough beads to make a bracelet that'll fit around your wrist comfortably. Beads that are six to eight millimeters are a good size for braclets and are readily available at craft and bead stores. Spend some time making a pattern that you like and then thread it onto the cord. Secure it with at least two knots. For extra strength, you can put a dot of jewelry glue, such as E6000, on the knots. It will need twenty-four hours to cure. When the bracelet is finished, place it under the light of the Full Moon. Close your eyes and say, "As the light of the sacred Moon blesses this piece with courage and power, I'll wear it with pride, I'll do what I must, and my courage will grow by the hour. So mote it be." Let it sit under the light of the Moon for at least one night. Wear it with power the next day and any day you are taking on challenges.

6
of Wands

Key concepts: Victory, attainment, recognition, success

The Six of Wands is an incredibly positive card in the tarot. It's the "Heck, yes, go for it" and "What are you waiting for?" card. You're going to be recognized for your efforts, so enjoy your time in the spotlight and make the most of it. Even if complete success is a way off, this card shows that all of the progress you've made and the continuing effort you're putting in is going to be worth it. While there are elements of popularity and social status connected to this card, the belief you have in yourself is the most critical element to your success.

Be Victorious Spread

There is nothing wrong with wanting to win in life. We all have different visions of what success looks like and are all on different journeys. If you've entered a competition or are up for an award, the Six of Wands tarot spread can give you that competitive edge. You may as well know what you're up against and everything you can do to ensure success.

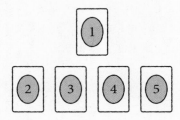

1. What do I need to know about the competition?
2. Are there any new skills I need to learn for victory?
3. Where do I need to be more consistent?
4. What do I need to stop immediately?
5. Who can I work with to achieve victory?

Victory Spell

The Victory Spell for the Six of Wands is perfect for when you're working on achieving something big. Whether you're training for a marathon, preparing for a sporting event, or undertaking a large creative project, this spell will turn you into an energetic magnet for success.

Best time to cast: New Moon

You will need

- Gold candle and holder
- Lighter or matches
- A small golden trophy with a blank writing area
- Gold paint pen or permanent marker
- A tumbled piece of pyrite

Light the gold candle. Write your name and date of birth on the inside of the cup of the trophy. Write your goal on the base or plate of the trophy. This needs to be done in the present tense as if you already have the award or success—for example, *first place in a marathon* or *sold-out gallery opening*. Place the pyrite in the cup, which is a stone of success and prosperity. Hold your hands over the trophy, close your eyes, and envision it being enveloped in golden light. Feel it hum with energy. While you do this, say, "I claim victory, I've won the day, victory is mine, without delay. So mote it be." Leave the trophy on your altar or in a safe place until your goal has been achieved. Allow the candle to burn down if you can.

7
of Wands

Key concepts: Boundaries, defensiveness, standing your ground, assertiveness

Even though this card can appear to be off-putting, there are a lot of positive influences in the Seven of Wands. You have more going for you than working against you. It's all about choosing what is worth protecting. What you really love and believe in is always worth protecting. Your boundaries are going to be tested throughout your life, so it's a good idea to fortify your protective magic regularly.

What Needs Protecting? Spread

If you're feeling a little off or feel that someone in your life is a bit of a threat, the tarot spread for the Seven of Wands is just what you need. When it comes to protection, try looking at multiple angles so that you're not leaving any gaps in your energetic armor. Working with this spread can give you the ability to rise above your worries and get a clear perspective.

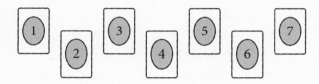

1. What is the best way to protect my energy?

2. What is the best way to protect my heart?

3. What is the best way to protect my mental space?

4. What is the best way to protect my family and friends?

5. Where in my life do I need to be more assertive?

6. Which ally is really in my corner?

7. What apparent threat is just an illusion?

Mirror Protection Spell

Mirrors are powerful magical tools. The spell for the Seven of Wands, which uses a mirror, is one of my favorite spells for protecting a household from unwanted energies. It's best to place the mirror on the inside of your front door. Just make sure it's secure, as the front door gets a lot of use. The size of the mirror doesn't matter; even a small handheld mirror will work. The great thing about this protection spell is that it's effortless to do. If you have pesky housemates, place the mirror on the inside of your bedroom door.

Best time to cast: Waning Moon

You will need

- Round mirror
- Black and white paint
- Paint brushes

Paint the back of your mirror black and allow it to dry. Suppose you want an extra boost and can proudly show a pentacle in your environment; once the black paint is dry, paint a white pentacle on the back. The pentacle is a protection symbol that is a well-loved and often used symbol for magical practitioners. When everything is dry, secure the mirror to your front door with the reflective glass facing the door. Trace the pentacle design on the mirror with your finger, and say three times, "Only love may enter here." Any unwanted energies will bounce off the reflective mirror surface and won't come into your house.

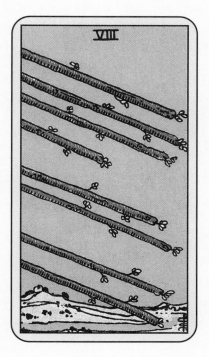

8
of Wands

Key concepts: Swiftness, speed, movement, momentum

Movement surrounds the Eight of Wands; when it arrives in a reading, it is time to act. This card is a welcome and exciting change for situations when you feel stuck or are waiting for an upcoming trip. This is a positive card for anyone who is working toward a goal. Quick decisions and change are also part of this card, so expect the unexpected and hold on to your undies for the ride to come.

Bust through Blocks Spread

There is nothing more frustrating than being hit with a roadblock. The Eight of Wands is the perfect card to remove anything that's standing in your way so that everything flows again. The tarot spread is meant to help you face the block head-on, so there's no time to ignore the messages delivered via this reading. The sooner you deal with what's holding you back, the sooner you'll progress again.

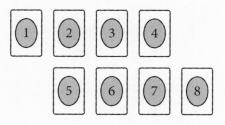

1. Why is my progress being halted?
2. What belief or action is blocking me?
3. Are there any unseen forces working against me?
4. How can I bust through this block?
5. What do I need to break through?
6. In what direction should I aim my energy and effort?
7. What do I need to release?
8. What am I learning through all this?

Smooth Move Spell

The tarot spell for the Eight of Wands will ensure that your moving day will go smoothly the next time you have to move. Moving is stressful; there are so many factors that you can't control, and so much can go wrong. These charms will be placed in important locations during your move. This small, easy-to-make charm protects your items from being misplaced or broken.

Best time to cast: Twenty-four to forty-eight hours before you move

You will need

- Ginger root
- Knife
- Cutting board
- Paper towel
- Black Sharpie

Cut the ginger into slices that are approximately one inch thick and pat them dry with a paper towel. Leave them overnight to dry a little on the paper towel. The next day, write the symbol for Jupiter, the planet associated with luck, on each of the slices with the black Sharpie. Ensure the symbol is on both sides. Place these charms in the vehicles you're using for the move, your old location, the new location, and on boxes that have breakable items. You may not have access to the new place you're moving to before the day of the move, which is fine; place one of these smooth move charms in the new location when you access it for the first time on moving day.

9
of Wands

Key concepts: Perseverance, resilience, weariness, final stand

You're almost there! It's been an undertaking to get where you are, and the effort hasn't always been fun, but you haven't given up. This card holds the message of long-term effort and pacing yourself so you get to the finish line. Sure, you're going to need a moment to regroup, catch your breath, and try a different strategy, but then it's back into the fire to finish the job.

Why Am I So Exhausted? Spread

If you feel like you've run a marathon most days, it's likely that you have more than one thing that's weighing you down and sapping your energy. The Nine of Wands tarot spread can help you find out what's contributing to your exhaustion. A tarot reading is never a substitution for health support from a medical professional. It can, however, be complementary and give you a new perspective on positive steps forward.

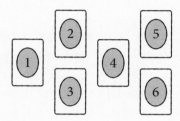

1. What is the state of my energetic defenses?
2. What strategy do I need to implement today?
3. Which person/situation do I need to block out?
4. What healing practice will energize me?
5. Which ally is going to help evaluate my work?
6. Do my guides have any advice on my energy levels?

Energy Recovery Elixir

This magical elixir is a favored way to help your immune system to do its job. All of the beautiful sunny ingredients with high vibration will help you recover your energy quickly. Don't underestimate the importance of listening to your body when you're taking on a lot. Even if you have to keep on going, like the figure in the Nine of Wands, having supportive foods and vitamins can make a difference. You can make this in larger quantities as long as you store it in an airtight jar in the fridge. It's best to drink this elixir within forty-eight hours of making it. You can also adjust the ingredients to suit your tastes. Want something sweeter? Add another orange. Want it a little spicier? Add a bit more ginger.

Best time to cast: **Anytime**

You will need

- Juicer or blender
- Two small oranges
- Two small lemons
- One-third cup chopped fresh turmeric
- One-third cup chopped fresh ginger
- One-eighth teaspoon of fresh cracked black pepper
- Fine mesh strainer or cheesecloth
- Bowl
- Vitamin D drops
- Glass jar or bottle with lid for storage

Add the orange, lemon, turmeric, and ginger to your blender or juicer. It's up to you whether or not you want to peel the oranges and lemons. Some machines will require it, so check the model's recommendation. If you're using the rinds, invest in organic oranges and lemons. If you need to, add a little bit of water to the mix to help with the blending. Add the fresh cracked black pepper. When everything is smooth, strain the mixture into the bowl through the strainer or cheesecloth. A good serving size is a large shot glass size. Make sure you shake the elixir before you serve it. Just before you take your elixir, drop five to ten drops of vitamin D into it and drink. Store the rest in your jar in the fridge.

10
of Wands

Key concepts: Overworking, burdens, responsibilities, obligations

I don't know about you, but I wouldn't want to trade places with the figure in the Ten of Wands. The task they're undertaking looks like stressful, hard work. It begs the question, "Is there an easier or better way to do this?" and the answer is always yes. This card is often associated with taking on extra responsibilities and other people's work. The work will be done, but it could lead to burnout.

Delegate It, Stubborn Spread

The Ten of Wands tarot spread is for the control freaks out there. You know who you are. You don't need to do everything, and it's more detrimental to your overall well-being than you may realize. So, if you're faced with a huge undertaking but aren't sure what you should do yourself and what you can let others assist you with, use this spread and start to let other people help you.

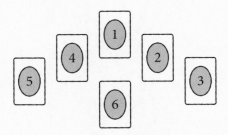

1. Why am I struggling to delegate?
2. What do I actually need to do myself?
3. What do I need to give to someone else?
4. What skills does that person have to possess?
5. How can I best support that person?
6. What will be the result of the work/project?

Let Go of Control Spell

If you need extra support to calm your control issues, the Ten of Wands spell is made just for you. There's nothing wrong with being independent and capable. However, it becomes a problem when you run yourself into the ground because you can't delegate or let it go. Not only is this spell easy and effective, but it's also bloody satisfying to do. By letting go of control, you'll create more space for new things in your life and time for self-care.

Best time to cast: **Waning Moon**

You will need

- Play-Doh or modeling compound
- Ten blank popsicle sticks
- Black marker or pen

Create a ball with the Play-Doh. Write something you're struggling to let go of on each of the popsicle sticks. It may be something you don't like delegating at work or a personal obligation that's not your responsibility, but you take it on anyway. When you've written one, stab it into the Play-Doh. Continue this process with each of the popsicle sticks. Your playdough ball will look like a weird pin cushion by the end. When you're done, take a few moments to look at everything you're taking. It may be the first time you've seen it presented like this. When you feel ready to let them go, take a random stick out of the Play-Doh and say, while you snap it in half, "I'm letting go of my control over this." Do this with each of the popsicle sticks. If you're feeling extra sassy, you can say something such as, "I'm done with this!" Make sure you snap the stick entirely in two. If you have a fireplace, you can burn the sticks. Alternatively, you can compost them.

PAGE of WANDS.

Page of Wands

Key concepts: Energy, enthusiasm, curiosity, suggestion

The Page of Wands is a bundle of energy. They want to engage with the world around them and do so with all that they are. They know that there is so much potential out there. While they're open to other people's suggestions and can be swayed easily, they can adjust to changes quickly and have fun no matter what. The Page of Wands seems to express themselves creatively with ease and are incredibly curious.

Playful Soul Spread

The tarot spread for the Page of Wands is a simple three-card spread. Just like the Pages, we're keeping it uncomplicated. Being open is one of the gifts of this Page, so be open to the message of the cards and look at each card from multiple perspectives.

1. Why have I been so serious lately?
2. What does my inner child want me to embrace?
3. Where can I be more spontaneous?

Wonder Spell

The Wonder Spell will help you embody your inner child's playful side. It's another journey spell that will take you outside of your comfort zone and bring some spontaneity into your life. Small things can make a big difference, and getting back to some of the simple activities of childhood can bring wonder to the way you look at life again.

Best time to cast: Anytime

You will need
- A photo of yourself when you were a child
- A yellow envelope
- A dandelion flower or other yellow flower

Place the photo and flower inside the envelope and close it. Hold the envelope to your heart and say, "I call upon my childlike wonder to come back into my heart, for the joy and wonder in my life needs a restart." Feel or visualize the yellow energy surrounding you. Take the envelope with the flower and photo with you as you carry out one of the fun activities suggested. Jump in puddles the next time it rains. Blow bubbles at a park. Finger paint with wild abandon. Dress up in a costume and go grocery shopping. Jump on a trampoline. Swing on a swing set. Blow bubbles in a milkshake. Skip down the street.

Knight
of Wands

Key concepts: Adventure, passion, daring, enthusiasm

The Knight of Wands is ready for anything. They thrive in fast-paced environments and adapt well to change. They may not have a lot of life experience, but their charm and confidence can lead them to take on endeavors without thinking it through. They bring all of their passion to everything they do. Like all Knights, action is needed when this card comes up. It's a sign to carry on and charge ahead.

Find My Soul's Passion Spread

The tarot spread for the Knight of Wands can be helpful when trying to find your soul's passion. It's important to remember that your soul's passion may change as you grow in life. It's also important to embrace the journey. The more pressure you put on yourself to find your purpose, the harder it can be to actually find it.

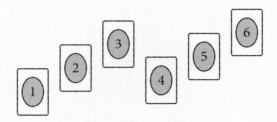

1. What is missing from my life?
2. What does my soul want me to explore?
3. How can I bring more passion into my life?
4. What gift do I need to share with the world?
5. How does my soul want to be expressed?
6. What are the first steps to embracing my soul's passion?

Winner Winner Spell

Want to win that drawing you entered for a free vacation? This is the spell for you. The Knight of Wands often comes up in readings about travel and adventures around the world. Naturally, you want their energy on your side when you enter these kinds of competitions. You'll want to say this charm while you enter and do the spell work after you've entered the contest or competition.

Best time to cast: At the time of entry and as soon as possible afterward

You will need

- Image of the destination for the competition
- Gold or green pen

When you enter the competition, chant, "Winner, winner, that's me, I'm going on vacation for free!" You can do this in your head or under your breath. After you have entered the competition, Google search for a common postcard design from that place. Print it out and write a postcard to someone you'd send one to while on that vacation, like you're enjoying your free trip. If you don't have a printer, you can go to a travel agency and get a brochure from the country of the prize and then collage a postcard with the images in the brochure. Place the postcard on your fridge.

Queen
of Wands

Key concepts: Magnetic, confident, optimistic, vibrant

The energy that comes from the Queen of Wands is warm and welcoming. They allow the right people and situations to come to them and rarely have to chase anything in their life. They know precisely what they are doing in every situation and can be a superb ally in business and social status.

This Queen doesn't back down when presented with competition. This Queen also adores attention and praise from others.

Is It All an Act? Spread

There is nothing worse than investing your time and energy with someone and then finding out they were leading you along. The Queen of Wands is a fantastic actor; they know how to get what they want and use this talent if needed. This tarot spread can be used for romantic, work, and creative relationships.

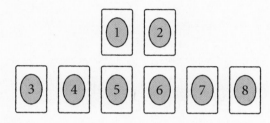

1. What is my real motivation?
2. What do I want to get out of this relationship?
3. What do I need to keep close to my chest?
4. Will I regret this relationship?
5. What are the risks of this relationship?
6. What are the blessings of this relationship?
7. What will I get out of the relationship?
8. What is the potential future of the relationship?

Reclaim Your Power Spell

The Queen of Wands radiates energy, which is a spell to use when you need to reclaim your power from people you've been giving it to. There is often a sunflower in the Queen of Wands tarot card. These flowers grow tall and proud. They can also grow on their own, standing firm. On the following page are a few suggestions for flower seeds you can use in this spell. Any of them will do the job. Enjoy nurturing your flower seedling as your energy comes back to you. Not only will these flowers be beautiful to look at, but they're also great for bringing pollinators to your garden.

Flower seed suggestions

Sunflowers: Blooms in summer and loves full sunlight

Marigold: Blooms throughout summer and fall and loves full sunlight

Coneflowers: Blooms in summer and loves full sunlight

Cosmos: Blooms throughout spring and summer and loves full sunlight

Best time to cast: New Moon

You will need

- Small pot
- Potting mix
- Tumbled obsidian stone
- Chosen flower seeds
- Water

Put a bit of potting mix in your pot. Place the obsidian crystal in the soil. Then, fill the pot with the potting mix. Plant your chosen seeds in a small pot. You don't want to crowd the pot with too many seeds. Give the seed a good watering, and say, "Grow and shine; I recall the energy that's mine." Gently place both hands over your solar plexus chakra, which is located a couple of fingers above your belly button. Close your eyes and envision glowing yellow energy and light pooling here. Feel the energy growing. When you feel your energy become powerful, say the following thirteen times: "I now recall my energy, my life force, my chi, back to me, may it flow gently back and bless me with vitality." When you're ready, open your eyes. Place the pot somewhere it will get a good amount of sun. If more than one starts to sprout, separate them out into their own pots or plant outside in spring.

King of Wands

Key concepts: Leadership, boldness, entrepreneurship, decisiveness

The King of Wands knows who they are and what their talents are. They often default to positions of leadership, and people readily follow their lead. Their energy can inspire others to help them with their vision and ideas. Whenever you sit in your power and carry out activities to help you know who you are, you embody the King of Wands.

Will I Be a Successful Entrepreneur? Spread

Not everyone is well-suited to be an entrepreneur. You need to be comfortable with taking risks, making decisions, and following through with your plans. The tarot spread for the King of Wands is perfect if you're thinking of stepping out and working for yourself. Even if you discover that being your own boss isn't for you, don't throw your passion and ideas out the window. You can make your dreams come true, as even entrepreneurs work with others to succeed.

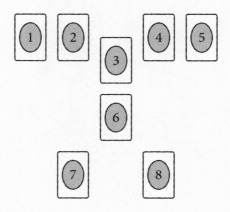

1. What kind of leader will I be?
2. Am I ready to be an entrepreneur?
3. What beliefs are holding me back from success?
4. Do I have the drive for success?
5. Is there a good market right now for my business?
6. What are the roadblocks I may face in business?
7. Who do I need to work with for success?
8. What is the advice for the future?

Step into Leadership Spell

Being a leader can be challenging, particularly if you're moving into a leadership position for the first time. The spell for the King of Wands is subtle, but it will support you every step of the way. You may need to adapt this spell depending on what kind of shoes you wear for work. To add extra energy to this spell, wear red or orange socks or underwear to work or paint your nails in those colors. Adding a little splash of colors associated with the King of Wands will sustain that energy throughout the day.

Best time to cast: **Anytime**

You will need
- Two small pieces of orange paper
- Orange or red marker

With the marker, copy the leadership sigil onto each piece of paper. Place the pieces of paper in your shoe either on top of or under the insole. You don't want the paper to make walking uncomfortable. The pieces of paper need to be small enough to put in your shoe under your feet or socks. You can also put the sigil directly on the insole of your shoes or in another area of your shoes. This sigil activates as you walk throughout your day as a leader. Replace as required.

Chapter 6
The Suit of Swords

I like to think of the suit of Swords representing the realm of the mind, intellect, and communication. Emblematic of conflict, clarity, and the power of ideas and beliefs, the suit of Swords challenges us to confront truths and navigate complexities through reasoning and sharp insight. This suit brings a direct, often brisk energy to reading, compelling us to address thought, communication, and decision-making issues without shying away from the more complicated aspects of life. An abundance of Swords in a reading typically indicates that the truth requires courage and honesty. Many of the cards in the Swords suit depict challenges or confrontations where you are being tested. The result of such tests is determined in the mind as much as by external forces. This suit wants you to examine how you can use your intellect and communication skills to achieve your goals. You'll also find your beliefs and ideas challenged as you evolve and learn new information. Swords can be used as an offensive weapon, the mighty pen, to communicate or to cut through confusion.

Ace
of Swords

Key concepts: Clarity, new ideas, breakthrough, inspiration

The Ace of Swords brings with it the winds of change and inspiration. This card holds within it the gift of clear thinking and keen intellectual abilities. Anyone stuck on ideas, writer's block, and mental clutter will find this card brings relief with its arrival. Having good ideas and cutting through the ones that will lead you nowhere is also connected to this card.

Find Inspiration Spread

The tarot spread for the Ace of Swords is perfect for those times in your life when you need inspiration. This could be for a project at work where a lot is riding on your success. Or you have a creative piece of work that's no longer feeling like it holds any magic.

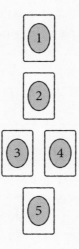

1. Why is my muse hiding?
2. How can I call my muse back?
3. What will bring me inspiration?
4. Where do I need to focus my mind
5. What new idea do I need to try?

Bust through Writer's Block Spell

Writer's block is the bane of a writer's existence, especially when there's a deadline looming. The tarot spell for the Ace of Swords is perfect for any writer. This talisman can be cast before you start a writing project to ensure you don't get writer's block or when the fiend decides to grace you with its presence.

Best time to cast: New Moon

You will need

- Yellow twine or leather thread
- Small clear quartz point
- A feather
- Glue (hot glue is recommended)

Using the twine or leather thread, tie the small quartz point to the feather's central shaft and secure it with a small amount of glue. Before you write anything, place this talisman near your keyboard or writing implements and say, "I call in the winds of inspiration, the words to flow, writer's block, I'll never know. So mote it be!" This writing talisman will work for you throughout the specific project you create it for. Keep it near your workspace until you've completed the work.

Spell Ingredient Law

Feathers have been important throughout history, from their connection to goddesses, gods, and angels to feathers being used as tools like quills. They're connected to the element of air and are wonderful ingredients for any magic-requiring messages. While each type of feather will have its own magical properties, you can use any feather for this spell. Please source your feathers ethically; not only will the source affect your spell, but as magical people, respecting our feathered friends is essential.

2
of Swords

Key concepts: Stalemate, decision, being on the fence, dilemma

The Two of Swords represents being stuck between a rock and a hard place. Often, the situations that accompany this card are made worse because it's being ruminated on over and over. You know you need to make a choice, but there is no clear indication of the best path. The way forward is to shut out other people's opinions, listen to your intuitive voice, and wait until the time is right to act on it.

Get Unstuck Spread

When you're not sure why you find yourself at a crossroads and unable to make a decision, use the tarot spread for the Two of Swords. Be ready to take positive action and remove any inner conflict that's been plaguing you. Sometimes, the best thing to do is nothing. You may find that the timing or circumstances aren't ideal.

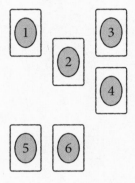

1. Why am I stuck?
2. What is the lesson of this situation?
3. What can I no longer avoid?
4. What action do I need to take to get unstuck?
5. What is the result of doing nothing?
6. What is the result of taking action?

Clarity Spell

Getting clarity can be a process, and the spell for the Two of Swords will get you there. You don't even have to remake the clarity bottle if you need clarity on something else. The critical thing about sand, glitter, or herb is that it won't dissolve in the water and will separate from it when given time to rest. I love glitter—I'm a regular magpie witch—but please use biodegradable glitter. Glitter is a horrible biohazard for waterways and animals. A fun, shiny, beautiful biohazard. It's been added here in this spell, as not everyone can access ocean sand or eyebright herb.

Best time to cast: Anytime

You will need

- Empty soda bottle or jar
- Water

- Ocean sand, biodegradable glitter, or dried eyebright herb
- Two small clear quartz points

Wash your bottle and remove the label. Place the sand, dried herb, or glitter in the bottle along with the two quartz points. Fill the bottle with water until it's at least three-quarters of the way full. Secure the lid and shake the shit out of the bottle while thinking about what you're confused about. When you feel like you've put your frustration and confusion in the bottle, put it down on a flat surface. Then go for a walk outside and leave your phone at home or at least don't look at any devices while you walk. You'll have your answer by the time you get back, and the water has settled.

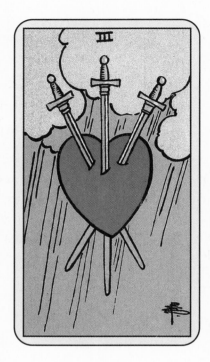

3
of Swords

Key concepts: Heartbreak, pain, division, betrayal

The Three of Swords imagery is clearly one of pain. It's never a welcome sign, but sadness can't be avoided in life, and loss will inevitably happen. The painful feelings we experience in life don't last forever, but they can feel like they're the end of the world when they arrive in our lives. This card also represents old patterns causing you pain, unresolved situations, and health issues that require surgery.

Listen to My Heartbreak Spread

The tarot spread for this card is designed to be used when you've suffered heartbreak and are tempted to run away from it. One of the essential elements of healing from loss is to take time to feel your emotions. While it's not recommended to carry this reading out while you're emotionally raw, when you feel ready to heal, use the guidance of this spread to help you in your heart's recovery.

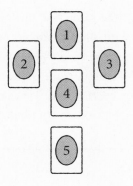

1. What is my heart telling me?
2. What do I need to accept?
3. How can I best express my pain?
4. What do I need to forgive?
5. What is the silver lining in this heartbreak?

Heal My Heart Spell

Please take your time when carrying out this spell and creating your heart-healing pillow. The image commonly used in the Three of Swords is a pierced heart, so making a whole heart full of healing magic is the perfect way to heal with this tarot card. This also makes a lovely gift to give a friend who's just gone through a bad breakup.

Best time to cast: Anytime

You will need

- Two pieces of red or white felt
- Scissors
- Red thread
- Needle
- Ribbon

- Rosemary,
- Heart's ease
- Dried lavender
- Chrysoprase tumbled stone

Cut two heart shapes that are the same size out of the felt sheets. Keep the scraps. Start to sew the hearts together with simple stitches around the edges. Feel loving and healing energy flow from you into the sewing, like you're mending a broken heart. When it's three-quarters of the way sewn closed, place the dried herbs, flowers, tumbled stone, and scraps inside the heart. Sew the heart closed. Tie the red ribbon around the heart with a bow. Give the heart a big hug and place it on your bedside table or under your pillow.

Art Magic Tip

Whenever you're making a pillow or poppet that requires stuffing, use a bit of glue around the edges of where you're going to sew. It will keep the fabrics lined up and also ensure that the herbs and crystals don't fall out. The sewing part of the spell is important; even if it's not perfect, it's about sewing your energy into what you're working on.

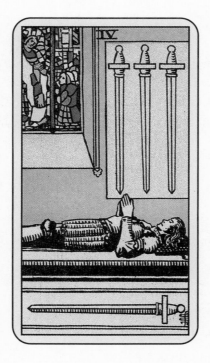

4
of Swords

Key concepts: Rest, contemplation, meditation, recovery

Everyone needs to rest from time to time because people aren't machines. The Four of Swords represents this essential part of life. If you don't listen to the message of the Four of Swords, the universe will put you on your ass involuntarily. Symptoms you need to find sanctuary include feeling overwhelmed, mentally overloaded and exhausted. Resting doesn't mean you're quitting. It means you know and respect yourself enough to recover from life's stresses and demands.

Inner Peace Spread

Give yourself the gift of untangling your stresses and intrusive thoughts with the tarot spread for the Four of Swords. Even if you receive cards in the reading that don't seem to make sense at the moment, remember that everything in your health is connected. Reflect on the cards you receive and allow the wisdom of the tarot to help you find peace.

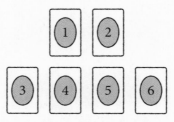

1. What do I need to say no to?
2. How do I relieve my stress?
3. How do I restore my mental peace?
4. How do I restore my physical peace?
5. How do I restore my emotional peace?
6. How do I restore my spiritual peace?

Peaceful Sleep Oil

Making magical oils is a form of spellwork that you can use for many occasions. They also increase potency the longer they are allowed to mix together before use. Getting a restful sleep is restorative in so many ways. Anyone with insomnia will tell you what they've been willing to do to get a good night's sleep. The oil for the Four of Swords can help you get a peaceful, deep sleep.

Best time to cast: **Anytime**

You will need

- One empty essential oil bottle with lid
- Apricot seed oil (carrier oil)
- Small tumbled howlite stone
- Agrimony essential oil or dried herb
- Lavender essential oil or dried herb
- Valerian essential oil or dried herb

Fill the empty essential oil bottle half full with the carrier oil of choice. Drop in the small tumbled howlite stone. Add four drops of each of the essential oils or a pinch of the dried herbs. Secure the top of the oil bottle and give it a light shake. Place a few drops on a diffuser bead near your pillow or anoint it on your wrists before bed. Keep the oil out of direct sunlight and store it somewhere cool.

Crystal Magic Law

Howlite is a fantastic crystal to work with if you find your mind racing at night when trying to fall asleep. It will lend its qualities of a peaceful mind and calmness to the sleep oil. Sleep with a piece of howlite under your pillow for an extra boost.

5
of Swords

Key concepts: Defeat, bullying, harshness, conflict

There are no winners with the Five of Swords; even the person holding the swords in apparent victory hasn't really won. There are people who believe that the ends justify the means. However, the universe doesn't care about rationalization. The Five of Swords is also a reminder that you've made a choice of whether you want to get involved with gossip and under-handed tactics or if rising above petty arguments is best.

Stop the Arguments Spread

Arguments are exhausting, but you can't be in any relationship without there being dis-agreements. The tarot spread for the Five of Swords can help you navigate those times when conflicts keep coming up in your friendships, family, or partners. With the energy of this tarot card spread, it's vital to own where you've been contributing to disputes and give yourself space when needed.

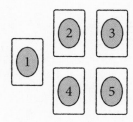

1. Why is this conflict continuing?
2. Where do I need to stand up for myself?
3. Where do I need to admit defeat and retreat?
4. Can this conflict be resolved in a healthy way?
5. What next empowering step can I take to aid in healthy conflict resolution?

F-Off Energy Vampire Spell

There are times when you need to draw a hard line in the sand and tell someone to fuck off. My F-Off Energy Vampire Spell is the spell for you if you want a versatile, nonmagical-person-proof protection spell jar. I even call it better than Buffy, and I love Buffy. This spell jar can be used at home, school, or work—anywhere you're having issues with nasty people.

Best time to cast: **Anytime**

You will need

- Small glass jar with lid
- Salt

- Three small black tourmaline crystals or smoky quartz
- Rice

- Rosemary dried herb
- Sage dried herb
- Lavender dried flower
- Basil dried herb

Layer the jar with the spell items in this order: salt, the tumbled stones, rice, herbs, and more salt. Secure the lid and take it to your place of work. Open the jar lid daily to ensure any bad vibes are attracted to the jar and not you. Your desk drawer is the best place to put this jar at work. Replace the contents of the jar every three to six months.

6
of Swords

Key concepts: Transitions, moving on, relief, progress

The Six of Swords is a welcome sight when you need safe passage in life. It can present itself as a person you can speak to in a safe space. This card brings with it peace after a difficult time in your life or even provides physical transport to somewhere more tranquil. The positive news is that things are moving forward, and you have an opportunity to make the most out of the relief.

Support in the Storm Spread

The tarot spread for this card is perfect to use when you feel lost in a turbulent situation in life and want to find peace and a safe harbor. Knowing where it's best to expend your energy and where you need to stop fighting and face what you may be trying to run away from can be valuable. As the Six of Swords is connected to the realm of the mind, never forget just how powerful your thoughts and words are in your daily life.

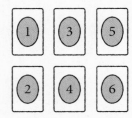

1. What can I do to help the storm clear sooner?
2. What can't I run away from?
3. Am I self-sabotaging my situation?
4. How can I bring more peace to my current situation?
5. Who is a safe ally to help me weather this storm?
6. What do I finally need to learn to get to a safe shore?

Travel Protection Spell

Not only does the Six of Swords spell create a sense of safety for when you're traveling, but it's also a talisman that you can take with you anytime you are away from home. You can even make one and place it in your car for protection.

Best time to cast: Anytime

You will need

- Small moonstone pendant
- Wing charm
- Jewelry making pliers

While you make this charm, say the following blessing: "Safe to travel, safe to roam, safety is mine, safe back home." Secure the wing charm to the moonstone pendant. The wings represent protective angelic wings that will envelop you safely and protect you while you travel. You can wear this protective talisman while you're traveling or you can place it somewhere in your carry-on. Have it with you the entire time you're traveling.

Crystal Magic Law

Moonstone is often connected to psychic abilities, but it's also said to bring protection to travelers. There are different colors of moonstone, and you can use any of these for this spell. Use your cage pendant and a tumbled moonstone if you can't get a pendant.

7
of Swords

Key concepts: Theft, dishonesty, risk, rebellion

When looking at the Seven of Swords, what has happened to the figure to have them in this position in the first place? Are they stealing something that's not theirs, or are they deep behind enemy lines, taking back what rightfully belonged to them? Every action and reaction has a story and perspective behind it, and the truth or what is right is not always so clear-cut. This is a card of warnings, at the very least. It's a call to listen, observe, and trust your gut when dealing with other people. The Seven of Swords can also be the card of someone who has no problem doing things their own way and forging a unique path.

Who's a Snake? Spread

One of the superpowers of the tarot is to tell you exactly like it is. Not what you want or may expect, but what is. The Seven of Swords tarot spread is a perfect way to find out if there is a snake in the grass. You've possibly started a new job and want to know who is genuine. Maybe you've found a new group of friends and want to ensure you're befriending the right people. Or you've been hearing gossip and want to know if it's bullshit or something you need to be worried about. For this tarot spread, you'll need to separate the deck into three piles: one of all of the major arcana cards, one of the sixteen court cards, and one with the remaining minor arcana cards. You won't use the minor arcana cards for this tarot reading.

Court Card 1: The Snake in the Grass: This card represents the person who is causing the most obvious problems. Maybe they're the loudest or most brash person in the situation.

Court Card 2: The Puppet Master: This is the real danger. They may be quieter and not outwardly dishonest, but be careful around this person.

Court Card 3: The Ally: The person you can trust. They may not be your new best friend, but they're not out to get you and will be safe.

Major Arcana Card 4: Action to Take: This is the card that will put you in an empowered position. It will show you a possible way forward as well.

Gossip Stopping Spell

Gossip is such a thief of time, energy, and joy. Sure, we all love a little bit of gossip; we can't help it, being social beings, but there are times when it becomes harmful and way too much. This is a go-to spell of mine to stop people from gossiping or spreading untrue rumors about you. It's easy and effective and feels darn good when small-minded people shut up! Freezer spells have been used by magical practitioners all over the world for a very long time; this is my spin on them.

Best time to cast: **Anytime**

You will need

- Small piece of paper
- Black pen
- Small plastic container with lid
- Small tumbled piece of black tourmaline
- Three teaspoons of milk thistle herb
- Water

Write the name of the person you want to stop gossiping about you on the piece of paper. Strike a line through their name. Fold the paper up and place it in the container with the piece of black tourmaline, the milk thistle, and the water. Stir it with your finger counterclockwise while saying, "Your meddling, gossiping days are done; I freeze you out, with harm to none." Secure the lid on the container and put it in the freezer. If you need to shut up a group of gossiping troglodytes, make a freezer spell container for each one. Don't remove them from the freezer.

Herb Magic Law

Milk thistle is also known as blessed thistle and is used in magic as an herb of protection. It's excellent for removing bad energies that you're worried may have attached to you.

8
of Swords

Key concepts: Restriction, limitation,
indecisiveness, martyrdom

There is a sense of helplessness with the Eight of Swords. You're stuck and
don't feel like there is a heck of a lot you can do to move toward a better
situation. The figure in this card is often bound and surrounded by swords

at low tide, stranded outside of a city with no one in sight to help them. While this may seem like a shitty situation, the positive side to this card is that you're the only person who can free you of the bindings holding you in place. This card holds the lesson of how our thoughts, habits, beliefs, and words can create a cage that we place ourselves in.

Free Yourself Spread

When you don't know how to get yourself out of the hole you've dug for yourself, climb out of the rut you're in, or want to banish the feeling of hopelessness, the tarot spread for the Eight of Swords is just what you need. You'll see and feel improvement just by making the decision to get back in the driver's seat of your life and take back your power and control. The most important thing about what you'll uncover with this spread is that you have to act on the guidance given. Do something about it when it resonates with you and shift that stuck energy.

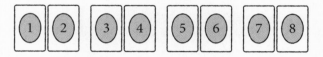

1. What habit got me here?
2. What belief is keeping me tied down?
3. What is the real reason I'm feeling trapped?
4. What fear appears to be real?
5. What new habit should I embrace?
6. What is the first step toward freedom?
7. What is the most likely future if I do nothing?
8. What is the most likely future if I free myself?

Cord Cutting Spell

Setting yourself free can be a scary thing. It's easy to get used to the routines, people, and reliable situations in life. The spell offering for this card is a plea to the universe to give you a boost of power. It's like having an energetic rocket up your butt so that you can no longer stay in your comfort zone. So, be prepared for change before you cast the spell.

Best time to cast: Waning Moon

You will need

- One white candle with a holder
- One black candle with a holder
- Candle carving tool or toothpick
- Plate
- Salt
- An eight-inch long piece of twine or natural fiber
- Lighter or matches

Carve your full name on the white candle. On the black candle, carve the name of the person or thing you want to be free from. If you're unsure of what you need freedom from, write the word *freedom* on it. Put the candles in the holders and place them on the plate. Wrap the twine around the top half of the candle's length. Secure it with some knots and ensure that the twine is taut enough that it holds its position, looping the candles together. Sprinkle the salt in a circle around the candles and the twine. Light both candles and allow them to burn down. The twine will catch fire, so make sure you have enough space around the plate so nothing catches on fire. As the string and candles burn, so will you be free. After the candles have burned down, bury the wax, twine, and salt by running water off your property.

9
of Swords

Key concepts: Nightmares, anxiety, stress, overwhelm

Anxiety, stress and fear suck. They can be debilitating emotions and make getting a good night's sleep almost impossible. This is the energy of the Nine of Swords. Sounds like a party, hey?! I have woken up in the middle of the night from highly vivid nightmares and have stared at the ceiling, unable to go back to sleep. It doesn't last forever, but that doesn't mean it's not dif-

THE SUIT OF SWORDS ✳ 213

ficult in the moment or that the effects don't linger. Getting the support you need during those times in your life and trying not to spiral too deeply, can ease the unwelcome feelings and help you sleep better, too.

Am I Cursed? Spread

There are times when there are outside influences at play, making your situation worse. I've lost count of the number of times I've had messages from people asking if they've had some negative magical working placed on them. In some cultures, religions, and spiritual practices, hexing and cursing are just as common as healings. If you don't believe you can be hexed, then you may never need this tarot spread. However, some people want to push their pain onto others instead of taking the time to heal themselves. These people may use manipulation as their weapon, and others may use magic. The Nine of Swords tarot spread is there for you if you ever wonder if forces are making your life harder and working against you.

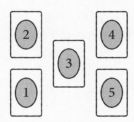

1. Why am I feeling repressed right now?
2. What is contributing to my feeling of being overwhelmed?
3. What unseen entities, allies, ancestors, or energy are affecting me?
4. What is the mundane action I need to take?
5. What is the magical action I need to take?

Banish Night Terrors Spell

There is something to be said for the power of dreams. Most people have no control over what happens when they fall asleep; some don't even remember their nightly adventures. This banishment spell is perfect for anyone who's having trouble getting a restful and peaceful night's sleep. You can carry out this spell if you're too stressed to sleep all the way to having sweaty night terrors. I've done this spell to help my son with his nightmares, and it's worked wonders.

Best time to cast: Anytime

You will need

- Two tumbled peach moonstones
- Two tumbled black moonstones
- One tumbled chrysoprase stone
- Lavender essential oil
- Sticky tack

Anoint the moonstones and chrysoprase with the lavender oil. Place one of the peach moonstones at one of the corners of the bed that needs protecting. This can be done at the bottom of the legs of a bed frame or bed base. Moving in a clockwise direction, place a black moonstone at the next leg, then a peach, and finally the black one. Place the chrysoprase either in the center of the grid under the bed or at the foot of the bed. You've created a magical crystal grid that will keep night terrors away. If the nightmares are pervasive, you'll want to cleanse your entire living space energetically.

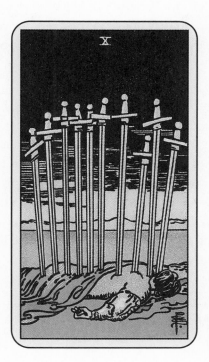

10
of Swords

Key concepts: Endings, betrayal, ruin, exhaustion

Just one look at the Ten of Swords, and you know there is no going back, there is no getting up, this is the end. It may feel bleak, but everything ends eventually. This card may manifest in your life as being so exhausted that you can't keep telling everyone that you're okay. It may be the end of a relationship that has been rocky for some time. It may also be the revelation that you've been betrayed. While these are some of the more complex lessons in life, there is something empowering about this card because you know whatever struggle you've been facing, it's over. The reality of that may not be desired, and the clean-up may be unpleasant and painful, but you now have all the important information you need to move on.

How Can I Let It Go? Spread

Trying to come to terms with sudden change or even to acknowledge something is over can be difficult. When significant time, energy, and investment have been put into something, letting go of it, even when it's over, can be tricky. This is where you can grab your tarot deck and use the Ten of Swords tarot spread. Letting something go is not a single-step process. There are days when it feels more manageable and days when you'll get sucked back into feeling let down again. It's okay and completely normal. Celebrate the wins when they happen, and give yourself grace when you're having a hard day.

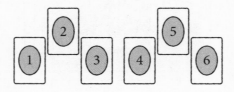

1. What feels unresolved within me?
2. What am I afraid to face?
3. Why do I want to hold on?
4. What do I need to take responsibility for?
5. What do I need to forgive myself for?
6. What is the positive aspect of this ending?

Negative Vibes Removal Incense

The spell for this card is a magical incense blend you can use to remove any bad vibes you feel around you or your living space. The Ten of Swords means that things are not great energetically, so working with clearing magic will help move things along in a positive way.

If you can't burn incense, you can substitute the resin and herbs for essential oils and make a spray or oil blend. It's recommended that anyone who frequently works with energy have a good cleansing routine. When it comes to the amount of each ingredient you need, it's best to start with a little of each and burn a sample to see how it mixes together. You can add a little more of some of your favorite ingredients as you go.

Best time to cast: Waning Moon

You will need

- Gum arabic
- Dried bay leaf
- Cedar wood chips or powder
- Dried rosemary
- Mortar and pestle
- Spoon
- Small glass jar with lid

Place a small amount of gum arabic, dried bay leaf, cedar wood chips/powder, and rosemary into the mortar and pestle. Combine the items and pour your energy into the blend as you do. When the blend is combined well, use the spoon to place the blend into the glass jar. You can burn this incense anytime you want to cleanse your space or remove any energetic swords you have on your back. This blend will be stored for a few months if kept in a dry room without direct sunlight.

Page of Swords

Key concepts: Curiosity, deduction, news, communication

The Page of Swords brings news, emails, contracts, and notifications. It's a welcome energy and card for anyone who's been patiently waiting to hear back from someone. This card may be a muse in your life that inspires you to create something new or try a new skill. Further education is also connected to this card. The Page of Swords doesn't sit still for long, however, so the thoughts you have may be fleeting or not manifest in something long-lasting if patience and perseverance aren't added into the mix.

What's Really Going On? Spread

When you want to know what's really going on in a situation you're involved with, the Page of Swords tarot spread is for you. It can be adapted to do third-party readings if you do them as well. When you're in a confusing situation or being told different stories from people, it can be hard to know what's really happening and what's utter bullshit. Well-informed means well-armed so that you won't be caught off guard or easily swayed.

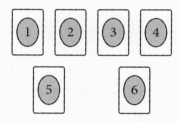

1. What's been hidden from me?

2. What lie or story have I been told to believe?

3. What is the hidden influencer?

4. What is the truth of the situation?

5. What is my role in that situation?

6. What is the best following action to take?

Reveal Your Secrets Spell

The Page of Swords loves information, and when you want to discover any secrets that are being withheld from you, this spell will be your best friend. The reveal oil you'll make for this spell can be used as an anointing oil for any applicable magic after its use. Just know any secrets you're keeping may also come out unexpectedly, so be prepared for that eventuality if you do this spell.

Best time to cast: New Moon

You will need

- Small glass bottle with lid
- Carrier oil; apricot kernel oil is great
- Small funnel
- Dried abre camino herb
- Dried cinquefoil herb
- Dried hyssop herb or essential oil
- Padlock with key

Fill the glass bottle to three-quarters with the carrier oil you've chosen. Then, add some of each of the herbs. Use equal parts of each herb for this oil. Secure the lid and give it a good shake. Anoint the padlock key with the reveal oil you just made. Unlock it and then lock it thirteen times. On the thirteenth time, open the padlock and leave it unlocked. Store your oil in an amber or blue glass jar and keep it out of direct sunlight and hot places.

Knight of Swords

Key concepts: Action, haste, directness, rash behavior

The Knight of Swords has no problem telling you what they think. They don't need an invitation or an opening to speak or defend what they believe in. There isn't a lot of forethought with this card, which can lead to unexpected surprises or people being unintentionally upset or hurt by words. The positive side to this card is that they will take the opportunities presented to them and run with it. This fearless confidence often serves the Knight of Swords well because they are quick-witted and can adjust as things change. There is a sense of urgency with this card. It's now time to take action. If you hesitate, you'll miss out.

Mending a Fractured Relationship Spread

The Knight of Swords is extremely good at saying exactly what's on their mind, whether they've thought it through or not. They can hurt people's feelings easily without meaning to. The tarot spread for this Knight is to help you mend a relationship that has started to feel strained. Not all friendships and relationships are meant to last forever; some ebb and flow because love isn't always easy. But if you want to try to reconnect with someone, this tarot spread may be a place to start.

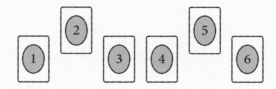

1. Where am I now in life?
2. Where is the other person now in life?
3. Is the relationship healthy for both parties right now?
4. What should the dynamic between us be if you reconnect?
5. What is my motivation for this reconciliation?
6. What is the future of the relationship?

Manifest My Ideas Spell

The Knight of Swords is fantastic at taking action. They're the perfect energy to embody when you want to manifest an idea you're passionate about. Most people in the magical world know what a vision board is. They work, and they're even more effective when you make them with magic. If you don't have the desire to make one physically, make a digital one in Canva and get it printed.

Best time to cast: **New to Full Moon**

You will need

- Picture of the Knight of Swords
- Pen
- Piece of plain cardboard
- Magazines, catalogs, and collage papers
- Scissors
- Glue

Write your full name, date of birth, and the Latin word *manifestus* on the back of the printout of the Knight of Swords. Create your magical vision board and ensure you put the Knight of Swords on the board. Any inspiring images or words that connect with your vision should be included. When the board has dried, place it somewhere you'll see it daily.

Art Magic Tip

Print media may not be easy to access for some people, so here are my tips on finding free or cheap resources for collaging: travel agency brochures, catalogs, thrift shop books, affordable second-hand books, and postcards.

Queen of Swords

Key concepts: Critical thinking, fairness, independence, wit

A word of warning: never underestimate a Queen of Swords. They may be all smiles and welcoming energy, but the second you try them or try to play them for a fool, you'll be in for a huge shock. The Queen of Swords is a card for being transparent with everyone around you. Clear boundaries, clear communication and being sure of your decisions. They will cut right to the heart of the matter, and while it may feel like it's a little harsh at times, this can be a gift. The Queen of Swords doesn't want you wasting time in this life, so they get right to the point.

Judge Judy Spread

No one knows how to tell it like it is quite like Judge Judy Sheindlin. There is the legendary Bianca Del Rio as well. Both are perfect incarnations of the Queen of Swords. They're quick with their comebacks, and nothing gets past them. The tarot spread offered for the Queen of Swords is here to give you some cold, hard truth. Be prepared to leave your bullshit at the door so you can hear what needs to be received and get on with your life. This tarot spread is excellent for when you think you're being too biased in a situation.

1. What is the energy I'm currently bringing to the situation?

2. How am I negatively contributing to the issue?

3. How can I positively contribute to the situation?

4. What do I need to stop making excuses for?

5. What do I need to take responsibility for?

6. What positive action can I take today to move forward?

7. What do I need to get over?

8. What opportunity is waiting for me on the other side of this?

Fairness Spell

I'm sure you've heard the sentiment "Life's not fair" at some point in your life. I know the first time I listened to this was from my parents. While this can be true, you can balance the scales a little to bring some fairness to a situation where you feel like you're not being appreciated or are getting the short end of the stick. This is perfect for when you need a fair outcome to any negotiation. Butterflies are a common symbol on the Queen of Swords tarot card. They are terrific magical allies for fairness, with balanced wings for flying and symmetrical patterns on their bodies.

Best time to cast: Full Moon

You will need

- Two small dishes
- Two blue butterfly stickers or images
- Twelve pebbles, tumbled stones, or coins

Place the two dishes in front of you. Put the butterfly image at the bottom of each dish. You don't need to stick the sticker on there. Butterfly stickers are just easy to source. Place one in each dish with the twelve pebbles and say, "One for you, one for me." Continue to do that with each pebble or stone until each dish has six pebbles. Hold your hands about an inch above each of the dishes. Feel or see universal energy flowing through you from your crown chakra and bathe the dishes and their content in this light. When you feel that enough energy has flown into them, say, "What's fair is fair, our even share, from this day on, we both have won." Keep these dishes on your altar until a fair agreement is reached. For an extra magical boost, wear butterfly jewelry when you're going through your negotiations. Touch the butterfly jewelry any time you feel the conversation is becoming unfair.

King of Swords

Key concepts: Intellect, affluence, analytics, ethics

The King of Swords is someone who appreciates logical thinking and intelligent choices. This is the card of being an expert in your field and higher education. This card comes up in readings when you must set emotions aside and look at things logically. There is an energy of detachment to this card, of not putting any expectations on others or being emotionally attached to the outcome. This is also a card of holding fast to your ethics and morals.

The Higher Lesson Spread

The tarot spread for this card is to be used when you're looking for the higher lessons in a situation. This is especially good if you need a big-picture perspective. It's an opportunity to get some wisdom from your higher self. The King of Swords often looks at the bigger picture when problem-solving. They look at different angles and the underlying connections and lessons at play.

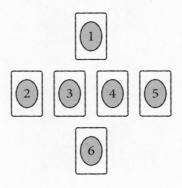

1. What is the karmic connection in this situation?
2. What does my higher self want me to know?
3. What is the logical tactic to take moving forward?
4. What is the mundane lesson to take from this situation?
5. What is the spiritual lesson from this situation?
6. What do I need to avoid next time?

First Choice College Spell

Getting accepted into highly prestigious educational institutions is a competitive process. The spell for the King of Swords can help you get into the college or university of your choice. Remember that sometimes when we don't get something you want. It's a blessing in disguise. If this spell doesn't work, know that the right opportunity will come to you.

Best time to cast: **Full Moon**

You will need

- Computer with printer
- Paper
- Envelope

Google an example of an acceptance letter from the college you want to be a student at. Create your own letterhead with the college's logo and the address of the campus you wish to study at. Canva is a helpful free tool for this type of work. Write your own acceptance letter with the created stationery. Ensure you put your full name and address on the letter and the date acceptance letters start to be received. Make it as official-looking as possible. Print the letter out, fold it, and place it in the envelope. Seal the envelope and put your name and address on it. Place it in the back of any education book you have.

Chapter 7
The Suit of Pentacles

The suit of Pentacles is a grounding force in the deck, deeply rooted in the material world and our physical experiences. It primarily deals with prosperity, work, material resources, and our environment. This suit reflects our relationship with the material realm and our bodies. The energy of the Pentacles is practical and nurturing, often suggesting a focus on achieving tangible results and building a secure foundation for the future. You want to work with this element to create things that stand the test of time, whether that is a lifelong career, a successful business, or a dream home to pass on to future generations. When the suit of Pentacles rules a reading, it indicates where pragmatic action is required and shows the rewards for consistent effort. This suit will show a querent the path to a secure financial future, the journey of health and vitality, and every step required to achieve desired outcomes.

Ace
of Pentacles

Key concepts: Prosperity, manifestation,
foundation, financial gain

Who doesn't love when new money or new financial opportunities come their way? This card holds the energy of the endless possibilities that can be created by the universe as long as the right conditions are met. The potential is fantastic, but it leads nowhere unless something is done to make it grow. This card is a sign that doors are going to open for you, and new resources will be offered to you soon.

Grow Your Abundance Spread

The tarot spread for the Ace of Pentacles is designed to help you maximize this new windfall and abundance. Sure, you could go out and spend it all in one shot, but you can also nurture it so that it grows even more prosperity in your life. Getting sound financial advice is also recommended for building a solid financial portfolio. Tarot and magic are great, but using all the tools available is just plain smart.

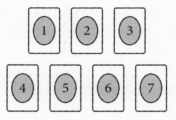

1. What will yield the best return on investment of my time?
2. What is the best use of the new money coming to me?
3. What do I need to stop doing to ensure I grow my prosperity?
4. What do I need to prepare for financially in the next three months?
5. What do I need to prepare for financially in the next four to six months?
6. What do I need to prepare for financially in the next seven to nine months?
7. What do I need to prepare for financially in the next ten to twelve months?

Unlimited Prosperity Spell

With this spell, you'll create a growing money altar for your space. It's so effective that I've been using it as part of my money practice and magic for years. If you want to take this spell to the next level, you can make your bowl or dish or paint a blank one. This also allows you to paint symbols of prosperity onto the dish. Any green dish will do if you can't make one from scratch.

Best time to cast: Start this spell at the New Moon and keep it going after that.

You will need

- Green cup, bowl, or dish
- One piece of tumbled pyrite
- One tumbled tiger's eye
- One tumbled green aventurine
- One tumbled citrine
- One tablespoon of dried basil leaves
- One cinnamon bark roll
- Eight coins of any kind

Place the tumbled stones, cinnamon, and basil leaves in the green dish. Put the coins in the dish, and with your index finger of your right hand, mix the contents of the dish clockwise eight times. Eight is the number of victory and prosperity. Place the dish somewhere on your altar or somewhere safe. Place a coin on the ground or a lucky token every time you find it in the dish. When you add anything to the bowl, say, "Unlimited prosperity today, tomorrow, and forever is mine." Watch your money grow!

Money Magic Tip

Thank the universe and your money every time new money comes into your life. If you find a quarter in the grass, pick it up and say thank you. When you receive your paycheck, say thank you. When you book a new client, say thank you. This gratitude practice can change your relationship with money and bring so many more blessings into your life.

2
of Pentacles

Key concepts: Juggling, flow, balance, adjustment

Y ou have to be a resourceful person to be able to juggle modern life
unless you want to live in a cave somewhere without internet and inter-
personal interactions. Adapting and going with the flow are key elements of
growth. The Two of Pentacles represents those forces. True, lasting balance
is not permanently feasible as the universe constantly moves and changes,

but doing your best while progressing is a definite win. Recognizing that you will experience ups and downs in all aspects of your life is a lesson of the Two of Pentacles.

Work vs. Life Spread

There is nothing wrong with being dedicated to your work. Some people love their careers and their chosen work; others work a number of jobs out of necessity. Where we can start to get in trouble with our energy is when one takes over completely. The Two of Pentacles tarot spread is a reality check for where you've spent your most precious resources: time and energy. This isn't meant to minimize doing what you have to do to pay the bills. As a responsible adult, there will be times when you need to be seriously focused on an issue or a project. The spread is meant to ensure you have the insight you need to get ahead and take change in stride.

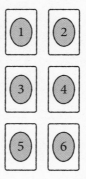

1. What do I need to prioritize?

2. What is a waste of time?

3. Where do I need to be more flexible?

4. What area of my life needs more harmony?

5. What change is coming?

6. How can I get the most out of this change?

Stop Saying Yes at Work Spell

Put your hand up if you've ever been so competent in your job that everyone comes to you to fix things. Keep your hand up if when you go away on holidays or are sick, you come back and no one has done a lick of work, and there is now a pile waiting for you. A lot of people do more in their jobs than they're being paid for, and it's so bad in some industries and companies that it's expected. While change in work standards doesn't happen overnight, you can empower yourself to stop taking on more than you can handle at work or at home.

As someone who used to work in the corporate sector in HR, I can also recommend that you have some statements ready to use at work when you don't want to take on more responsibility or are feeling pushback from a supervisor. Something along the lines of "Can you please let me know if this request is a top priority as I have a full workload right now? If it is, please instruct me on what I can delegate to someone else or work on later so I can do this task." Make your managers manage, not just dump shit on your desk and expect you to figure it out.

Best time to cast: **Waning Moon**

You will need

- Small tumbled citrine or clear quartz
- Empty essential oil bottle
- Orange oil or dried orange peel
- Ginger oil
- Pine oil
- Sandalwood oil

Make your power oil blend. This recipe is adapted from a Scott Cunningham recipe. Place the crystal and a small amount of orange peel in the empty oil bottle. If you're not using orange peel, put five drops of orange oil in the bottle. Then, add three drops each of ginger, pine, and sandalwood. Put the lid on and mix by shaking.

Take the bottle of oil and go to a mirror in your house. Anoint your wrists with the oil, close your eyes, and allow the oil's aroma to fill your senses. When you're ready, open your eyes. Look yourself in the eye in the mirror and say, "I'm unable to help you right now," or "No." Any affirmation of putting professional boundaries in place will bring the right energy and activate the oil. This spell works better the more you say the boundary affirmations. Practice makes progress. Anoint yourself with the oil at work when you feel like your professional boundaries are being tested.

Anointing Oil Tip

Always test any oil you intend to put on your skin for allergic reactions. You'll only ever need to use a small amount of oil. A little goes a long way.

3
of Pentacles

Key concepts: Collaboration, assessment,
planning, contribution

There's nothing worse than working on a team project and being the only one doing anything. We've all been there, and it's frustrating, to say the least. The energy of the Three of Pentacles is ideal in teamwork situations. Everyone brings their skills and perspectives to the table to create something lasting and more significant than the individual can produce alone. Sometimes, in the process, you take on a mentoring role where you teach new skills; other times, you learn from someone else. Any situation that sees you growing your skills is connected to the Three of Pentacles.

Long-Term Plans Spread

The tarot spread offered for the Three of Pentacles is perfect to do before you undertake any project that's going to require a lot of work and resources. I don't know about you, but I'd prefer to know if something will be a waste of time. Ultimately, you have to make the decision that feels right, but at least you can go into the next significant undertaking of your life with clear insight.

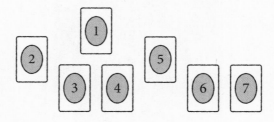

1. What is the current energy around this plan?
2. What is the long-term physical cost of this plan?
3. What is the long-term emotional cost of this plan?
4. What is the long-term mental cost of this plan?
5. What is the long-term outcome of the plan?
6. What do I need to reconsider with this plan?
7. Is this plan aligned with my highest good?

Work Together Well Spell

Working well with others isn't always easy. Clashing personalities and motivations can cause issues. Each person also has their strengths and weaknesses that they're bringing to the table. The spell for the Three of Pentacles brings some of my favorite things together:

baking and magic. You can use your favorite recipe for chocolate chip cookies, banana bread, or any recipe you can add three types of chocolate chips or nuts to. There's no better way to start off a project or team collaboration than with some baked goodies! Just make sure you check if anyone has any allergies before you bake.

Best time to cast: Anytime

You will need

- Your favorite cookie or banana bread recipe and ingredients
- Three types of chocolate chips or nuts or a mix

Prepare your dough. When you get to the step where you add the chocolate chips or nuts, select the first one and as you add it to the mixture, say, "May we work together with harmony and productivity." Select the next one, and as you add it to the mix, say, "May we communicate clearly and come together daily." Then select the final nuts or chocolate chips, and as you add them to the mixture, say, "Strength to strength, step by step, we work together, challenges we intercept. We blend and mix and create, the work is done, it's something great." Bake your cookies, take them to work, and share them with the people you're working with.

4
of Pentacles

Key concepts: Withholding, saving, possession, financial control

There are often a lot of negative associations with the Four of Pentacles, and yes, the card does mean hoarding and being overly frugal. However, this card also reminds us to have clear boundaries with our finances. There's nothing wrong with desiring financial stability and doing what you can to ensure it. There's nothing wrong with saying no to people when they want to borrow money and being wise with your investments. This card's energy is one of prudence with one's resources, and that's a practical way to be. Where it can be damaging is when the withholding harms you or others. That's when readjustments and growth need to take place.

Stop Money Leaks Spread

If you want to understand why money seems to fly out the door as soon as you get it, this tarot spread is for you. Combining money and spirituality has so many hang-ups and judgments. We're unaware of some of the beliefs and actions contributing to money leaks. Of course, when the Four of Pentacles arrives in our lives, it calls for us to get a budget, too!

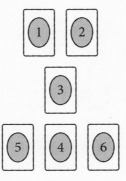

1. What is the lesson I'm learning about money?
2. What am I learning about boundaries?
3. What do I need to stop doing with my money right now?
4. What do I need to start doing with my money immediately?
5. Where's the most significant money leak coming from?
6. How can I stop the money leak?

Get My Money Back Spell

Asking people for money back after it's been loaned out is very stressful for many of us. Maybe it's because we were never taught to have conversations about money in our houses, or we don't want to seem "mean." This spell can help you get your money back sooner. Sure, you may still have to put on your adult pantaloons and have the conversation, but you'll also have the universe at your back, ensuring the outcome is in your favor.

Best time to cast: New Moon

You will need
- A small piece of paper and a green pen
- Two tumbled lodestones
- Green twine or elastic band

Write the name of the person who owes you money on a piece of paper. If you know the exact amount, put that on there too. Write the jera rune on the paper as well. This is the Elder Futhark rune that represents harvest and yield. Fold the piece of paper and place it in between the stones. The magnets will lock it in and bring it together. Secure everything with green twine or an elastic band. Put the bundle in your bag or purse. For bonus magic, put on "Bitch Better Have My Money" by Rihanna. Hold the bundle, put all your energy into it, and then place it in your bag or purse.

Crystal Magic Law
Lodestone is a naturally magnetic crystal that means "leading stone." It's an ideal crystal to use in any spell where you need to bring anything to you. A powerful stone of attraction, it's also a grounding stone that will bring money to you.

5
of Pentacles

Key concepts: Poverty, financial hardship, exclusion, struggle

The Five of Pentacles is one of the least welcoming cards in the tarot. No one wants to be left out in the cold, struggling to get by. Being in a situation where you feel like the world is working against you and you can't get ahead no matter what you do is awful. This card may manifest as financial struggle and hardship in your life, or you may have just lost a job or group of friends. No matter the circumstances, things don't stay the same forever, and things will get better. Getting through the hardship and keeping the faith isn't easy. This is where the work with this card can keep you in the right headspace and start your fortunes changing for the better.

Hope in the Darkness Spread

One of my favorite lyrics of all time come from Rush's song "The Pass," written by the band's incredible drummer Neil Peart. Particularly, I love the lines that seem to pull from Oscar Wilde's play *Lady Windermere's Fan*: "We are all in the gutter, but some of us are looking at the stars."[1] This is the inspiration for the tarot spread for the Five of Pentacles. While you're feeling down and out, some spiritual support and perspective can see hope grow.

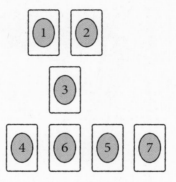

1. Which guide or ancestor wants to support my recovery?

2. How do I best work with this guide/ancestor?

3. Where can I find assistance in the physical world?

4. What is genuinely out of my control?

5. What can I control and change?

6. What excuses are standing in my way?

7. What is the first step to recovery?

....

1. Oscar Wilde, *Lady Windermere's Fan* (New York: Samuel French, Ltd., 1893), 77.

Be Debt Free Spell

To say that having debt is stressful is an understatement. It can feel overwhelming and hopeless, two energies connected to the Five of Pentacles. Instead of focusing on your money problems, working this magic shifts your focus to something productive and positive. This spell works with any debt, from credit cards to student loans. When you're working with money spells, try not to focus on how the money you need is going to make its way to you. When you try to rationalize how you're going to pay the debt, you're limiting the avenues the universe may use to give you the money you want.

Best time to cast: Full Moon or Waning Moon

You will need

- A small piece of paper and a pen
- Beeswax candle sheet natural or green
- Basil essential oil
- Cinnamon powder
- Candlewick
- Any bills that need to be paid
- Lighter or matches

Write the total debt you need to be free of on the piece of paper. Place the beeswax sheet face down with the smooth side facing up. Place a light layer of basil oil over the sheet (too much, and this will burn too quickly). Sprinkle the cinnamon powder on the sheet, again sparingly. Put the small piece of paper with the debt amount on the sheet. Now, place the wick on one edge of the sheet and roll the candle. Beeswax is naturally tacky, so it will roll and stay together well. Place the bills under the candleholder you're going to use while burning this spell candle. Light the candle and say, "Debt be gone, paid in full, now debt free, money I pull in. As I will it, so mote it be!" Allow the candle to burn down in a safe area. Make sure those bills don't get lit on fire!

6
of Pentacles

Key concepts: Generosity, charity, community, distribution

The Six of Pentacles holds the energy of sharing resources with others. It represents both sides of that exchange, being the one who gives and also the one who receives. It's the card of engaging with your community, being open with your knowledge and skills, and offering assistance to those who need it. It's a card of gratitude and kindness.

Build Your Self-Worth Spread

There is a direct link between your self-worth level and your relationship with money and the good things in life. If you've been told accepting something as small as a compliment is self-ish, how are you going to go for a promotion at work or have good boundaries with respect to your hard-earned cash? Having a healthy self-esteem can bring positive benefits to every aspect of your life. The tarot spread for the Six of Pentacles can show you where your blind spots are as regards your worth and what may be the source of feelings of low self-worth.

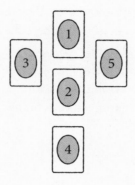

1. What gifts do I need to own fully?

2. How do I foster more kindness with myself?

3. What boundaries need mending right now?

4. What illusion do I have about myself that I need to drop?

5. What action do I need to take to foster a better relationship with myself?

Reach a Donation Goal Spell

The Six of Pentacles spell is a magical twist to the thermometer charts commonly used for funding goals. By having a working representation of the goal you have in mind, you're constantly sending it energy. This spell can be used whenever you're looking for community assistance for a charity or project. Working this spell is satisfying as it's an ongoing piece of magic. You'll be interacting with it every day that funding is open for contributions from donors.

Best time to cast: Full Moon or Waning Moon

You will need

- A glass jar
- Permanent green marker
- Sticker or image of the Six of Pentacles tarot card and tape
- Six gold coils or dollar bills
- Spoon
- Container with rice

On the glass jar, create measurement marks. By the top mark write the funding goal you have. The bottom mark is zero dollars. Then, put some figures next to the other marks you've made on the jar increasing in amount. On the other side of the jar secure the image of the Six of Pentacles tarot card with tape or adhere the sticker of the card on there. Place the six gold coins or dollar bills in the jar. As you do, say, "Money come and flow with ease, reach my goal, thank you and please." Every time there is a donation added to the campaign or charity, sing out, "Cha-ching, thank you!" and add some more rice to the goal jar. Continue to do this until you've reached your funding goal. If you go over, keep going!

7
of Pentacles

Key concepts: Investments, progress, fruition, results

Who doesn't love a bountiful harvest in their lives? The sense of accomplishment and success can be so sweet. However, waiting for it can be challenging. Having patience and pushing forward, even when things slow down, is one of the core energies of the Seven of Pentacles. This card is a reminder that progress is being made even if you can't see the results of your actions and hard work. Any growth, no matter how small, is growth all the same. There is also the need to assess and contemplate if there's a way to work smarter and not harder to get the desired results and then implement those changes as necessary.

Work Smarter Spread

The tarot spread for the Seven of Pentacles can be a great way to save precious time. Learning how to work effectively and effectively use your time and energy feels good, as well as being productive. This tarot spread doesn't pull any punches, so be willing to try new things and abandon tactics that are just not worth your time. Even if that feels like you're taking a step backward, you'll move three steps ahead later.

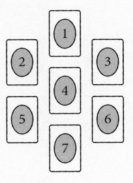

1. Where is the most significant opportunity to grow?

2. What's no longer working?

3. Where do I have to cut back?

4. How do I stop procrastinating on this?

5. What needs more time and effort?

6. What needs more nurturing?

7. What is the potential result of my labor?

Bountiful Harvest Spell

The Seven of Pentacles is connected with reaping what you sow, and this Bountiful Harvest Spell will ensure that all of your work will be worth it. A good harvest may represent good returns on your investments, a good return on money spent on your business marketing, or a good yield. Make it work for your specific situation. If pumpkins aren't in season, you can use a pumpkin-shaped candle.

Best time to cast: New Moon

You will need

- Small orange pumpkin
- Cutting board and knife
- A small piece of tumbled pyrite
- Orange or green candle
- Grapeseed oil
- Lighter or matches

Cut the top of the pumpkin off. Place the piece of pyrite in the small pumpkin. Anoint the candle with a couple of drops of grapeseed oil and secure it in the pumpkin. Light the candle and say, "A bountiful harvest is coming to me, abundance, prosperity I call, so mote it be." Allow the candle to burn down.

Crystal Magic Law

Pyrite is a perfect mineral to work within any business or money spell. Its other name is fool's gold, as it looks like real gold. It also has shielding abilities to protect your money and finances, which is a magical bonus!

8
of Pentacles

Key concepts: Mastery, craftsmanship,
effort, attention to detail

The figure in the Eight of Pentacles is doing the work and concentrating on the task at hand. They know what they're doing, and that comes from practice and patience. This card holds the energy of becoming a master at what you do through trial, error and time. You can't cut corners with this card when you really want something. Quality over quantity is also connected to this tarot card.

Is This Course Worth It? Spread

The tarot spread for the Eight of Pentacles is very helpful when you're looking at a new course, degree, or program that promises to level up your life. Higher education can be pricey, and make no mistake, the amount of money institutions put into getting your registration is mind-blowing. Knowing whether or not the course is going to be worth your time and money can help you avoid useless certificates and ensure that you are enrolling in the right programs with the proper outcomes. No matter what someone promises you, racking up vast amounts of debt for education is a surefire way to get stuck financially. If your vocation requires certification or a degree, that's completely different from wanting to do something because it's interesting.

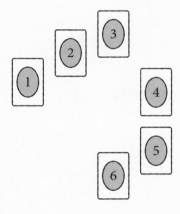

1. Is this institution/teacher aligned with my energy?

2. What effort is required to complete the course?

3. Will this course help me obtain my goals?

4. Are there any hidden costs or requirements?

5. What are the benefits of completing this course?

6. What general advice is there for my career development?

Get Your Promotion Spell

The spell for the Eight of Pentacles can be used when you're going for a pay rise or a promotion at work. It'll work for both situations. There's nothing wrong with casting some magic to aid you in leveling up your career. Magic is a tool, after all. Working in corporate HR for many years, I impart this negotiation technique to you. Print out your job description (often, it will be in your work contract), and if you're doing any duties that aren't in the job description, write them down and take that information into your negotiation. Look at the cost of living increases and what competitors are paying people at the same level as you. Arm yourself with information so that you can give concrete reasons why you deserve more money and that promotion.

Best time to cast: New Moon

You will need

- A printoff of the job description of the position you are going for
- Gold or green candle with candleholder
- Candle carving tool or toothpick
- Basil essential oil
- Lighter or matches

With the job description printed out in front of you, take the candle and carve your name into it along with the title of the position you're going for. Anoint the candle with a few drops of the basil essential oil. Place it in the holder with the job description under the candleholder. Light the candle and hold your hands on either side of the candle and say, "I call in what I am worth, the money, the title, and all of the perks. This promotion is mine and the pay raise, I claim this today, now spell get to work, so mote it be." Let the candle burn down if possible.

Magical Timing Tip

Magical timing doesn't always line up with real-world needs. If you need to cast this spell at a time that's not the New Moon, do it. It doesn't mean the spell won't work. Your desire, intention and real-world work will help the magic manifest.

9
of Pentacles

Key concepts: Wealth, success, financial independence, status

When you're living in the energy of the Nine of Pentacles, you can get anything you desire. Your basic needs are more than being met, and you're enjoying the finer things in life. This card often shows up when the querent has more than one stream of income or has come from money. It's a positive card when you're asking if a business or project is going to be successful, as it points to a HECK YES. It's the ultimate card of being self-reliant.

The Road to Financial Independence Spread

If you want to know how you can move toward financial independence, this tarot spread can help you identify your blind spots. If you find financial information as exciting as reading ingredient labels, partner this with a consultation with a financial advisor, specifically a fiduciary. Most banks will have free financial services you can utilize to be wiser with your cash.

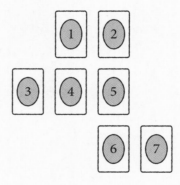

1. Where am I now financially?
2. What money strengths do I have?
3. What changes do I need to make regarding my credit?
4. What changes do I need to make regarding my savings?
5. What changes do I need to make regarding my investments?
6. What communication do I need to have about money?
7. What financial action do I need to take today?

More Clients and Customers Spell

The Nine of Pentacles spell is designed for when you want to level up your money game in a small or large business. You'll align yourself with the right clients and customers when you cast this spell. It puts out an energetic fishing line to the universe so you can bring the right clients in daily.

Best time to cast: New Moon

You will need

- Your favorite Nine of Pentacles tarot card
- Your phone

Take a photo of your chosen Nine of Pentacles card with your phone. Set it as your phone wallpaper and lock screen. Every morning before you start work, look at the Nine of Pentacles on your phone and say, "I effortlessly attract my ideal clients/customers to my business today." Remember to say thank you each time you get a new client. Having the Nine of Pentacles attached to your phone will attract this energy to you 24-7.

10
of Pentacles

Key concepts: Financial stability, inheritance,
material success, family values

This card is the culmination of long-term financial plans and positive actions. The Ten of Pentacles represents solid foundations in all areas of career, family and money. This is a positive card in most situations, as protection and resources are available to anyone connected to the card. This energy may manifest as receiving an inheritance, access to savings or having enough to fall back on if needed. Outside of money, this card has emotional and physical support—a place where you feel at home.

Financial Stability Spread

The tarot spread for the Ten of Pentacles is a financial roadmap to bring financial stability to your life. You can carry out this spread any time; you don't have to wait for a New Year or New Moon to do it. It is a spread of action, so ensure you come back to it and reflect on what is working and what is not. Did you get off track for one month? No problem. Just get back into alignment and pick up where you left off. It's a big spread, so take your time with it.

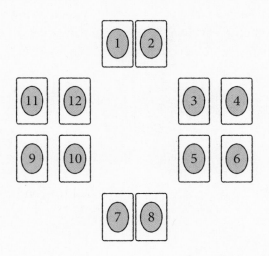

1. Month 1: What is the Money Energy for this month?

2. Month 1: How do I make the most of it?

3. Month 2: What is the Money Energy for this month?

4. Month 2: How do I make the most of it?

5. Month 3: What is the Money Energy for this month?

6. Month 3: How do I make the most of it?

7. Month 4: What is the Money Energy for this month?

8. Month 4: How do I make the most of it?

9. Month 5: What is the Money Energy for this month?

10. Month 5: How do I make the most of it?

11. Month 6: What is the Money Energy for this month?

12. Month 6: How do I make the most of it?

Find the Perfect Home Spell

Finding the perfect home to buy or rent can be time-consuming and arduous. The stress that comes with finding housing can feel all-consuming. The spell for the Ten of Pentacles is perfect for when you want that dream house to live in. Even if everyone else says it's not going to happen, you can create a reality where it manifests for you and your family. Trust your gut whenever you enter a new space. It may look good on the surface, but the energy may feel off. Your intuition always knows. When sourcing a key for the spell, it's advisable to use a charm or ornate key, not an old house key. Old house keys are attached to a specific property.

Best time to cast: **New Moon**

You will need

- Printed map of the neighborhood you want to live in
- Piece of paper
- Gold pen
- A key
- Gold ribbon

Lay out the map of the neighborhood in front of you. On the piece of paper, write down your name, the requirements of the house you need (number of bedrooms, bathrooms, pets allowed, etc.) and the maximum amount of rent or price of sale you have in your budget. Roll up the piece of paper, the map, and the key in a tight roll and secure it with the gold ribbon. Say, "The house of my dreams is already mine; I call it, I claim it, accept it, it divinely aligns. As I will it, so mote it be." Keep it somewhere safe in your current home. Take it to your new home when you have it and say thank you. Keep the key somewhere in the new house.

Page
of Pentacles

Key concepts: Simplicity, kindness, routine, good news

The Page of Pentacles has a deep connection with the natural and material world. Things they can put their hands on make sense, and they like life to be uncomplicated. Thriving in a routine and remaining open-minded are also connected to this card. As with all Pages, they're the bringer of news.

This Page will bring tidings of job opportunities, income streams and fixes you've been looking for.

Keep It Simple Spread

In keeping with the theme of simplicity, the tarot spread for the Page of Pentacles is a three-card, no-nonsense one. Just because a tarot spread isn't fifteen cards doesn't mean it's not profound and effective. This is a tarot spread to use when you're confused about a solution or are finding solutions too complicated to grasp. Sure, this tarot spread isn't going to solve algebra equations, but it will get you out of your own head.

1. Why am I complicating things?
2. What's trying to distract me?
3. What is the obvious solution?

Heal a Sick Animal Spell

The spell for this card is connected to the Page of Pentacles' love for animals. You can carry out this spell for your pets who may be unwell or any animal you know that needs healing in their lives. Adding this to the spell is perfect if you have experience with Reiki or energy healing. The great thing about this animal healing spell is that you don't even need to be in the same place as the animal. A photo or picture is all you need.

Best time to cast: New Moon to Full Moon

You will need

- Photo of your pet or the animal that needs healing
- Green ribbon at least twelve inches in length
- Three adhesive bandages
- One green envelope
- Dried thyme herbs

Take the photo of the animal, and on the back of the photo secure one end of the green ribbon with the bandage. Then start to wrap the ribbon around the photo while chanting, "Precious animal, may you heal, completely and fully, renewed you feel." Do this until your photo is wrapped in the ribbon. Secure the other end of the ribbon with another bandage. Sprinkle your dried thyme into the green envelope and then place the wrapped photo inside. Use the final bandage to seal the envelope. Place it somewhere safe. Your altar is perfect. You can put your hands on the envelope daily and send love and healing until they're well.

Knight of Pentacles

Key concepts: Reliabile, hardworking, productive, conservative

The Knight of Pentacles is a doer, and when they've set their mind to completing something, they're going to ensure it's done. This card holds the energy of the value of a job well done and a day of productivity. It's also a reminder that small steps are worth celebrating, not just the big ones. It's in focusing on the next small step forward that we make lasting change and something long-standing. This card represents reliable people, even if they're a little predictable.

Am I Being Stubborn or Determined? Spread

There can be a fine line between being determined and being downright stubborn. This tarot card is connected to the zodiac sign of Virgo, the perfectionist of the astrological signs. Perfectionism can be debilitating and mask itself as being determined. The tarot spread for this card will tell you directly whether you need to dig in or get out.

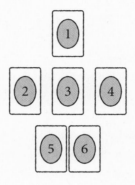

1. Why don't I want to give up control?
2. What am I really fighting for?
3. What is the cost of taking this stance?
4. What is the outcome of my defiance?
5. Where do I need to be more flexible?
6. What is the best step forward?

Protect My Energy Necklace

If there were any of the Knights in the tarot I would want to have to protect my energy, it would be the Knight of Pentacles. Sure, they're not the most flashy, but they'll stick by your side through thick and thin. The spell for this card calls this energy to you and envelops you in protection. It's like having this Knight by your side energetically at all times.

I wear my Knight of Pentacles necklace at any event or workshop, so I stay grounded and protected at all times. If you're unable to source gemstone beads, black glass beads are great substitutes.

Best time to cast: Waning Moon

You will need

- Black silk thread
- Scissors
- Tape
- Pentacle charm
- Six millimeter smoky quartz beads
- Six millimeter hematite beads
- Six millimeter black jet beads
- Silver or gold lobster clasp
- Jewelry glue or E6000

You'll need enough beads to make a necklace that's a comfortable size. If you don't want to create a necklace with a clasp, ensure the thread and number of beads are enough to put the necklace easily over your head.

You'll also want a medium-thick silk thread; if it's too thin, it won't support the beads' weight and will break easily. Black is the color of protection, but you can also use white.

Placing some knots next to a small grouping of beads will save most of your gemstone beads if the thread wears and breaks. You can then make another one without losing all of the beads.

Measure out the black silk thread so it's the desired length you want for your necklace. Add three to four inches to that length and cut the cord. Tape down one end of the thread. While you're threading on the protective gemstone beads, place your intention of shielding and grounding into the necklace and beads. You can play with the design before you start to string it. Any design or quantity of each bead will do. At the mid-way point, add the pentacle charm. Continue to bead the rest of the necklace. When you're happy with the design, secure each end on the clasp or with knots. You can place a little drop of jewelry glue on the ends for extra strength. Allow the glue to dry completely before you put it on. You now have your Knight of Pentacles with you when you wear it.

Pentacle Symbol Law

Pentacles and pentagrams have been misused in many ways in popular culture. It's not an evil symbol at all. It's actually a magical symbol of protection. It's associated with the element of earth, so it's perfect to use when protecting yourself in this material realm.

Queen of Pentacles

Key concepts: Healing, nurturing, welfare, homebody

The Queen of Pentacles knows just how important it is to have a welcoming home environment. They're concerned with how people feel and how they're taking care of themselves. While most of these wonderful people put everyone else first, when this card comes up, it's an important nudge to take care of yourself.

How Can I Heal? Spread

True healing requires a holistic approach. All of our systems work together, and so should our recovery. The tarot spread for the Queen of Pentacles is designed to look at your mind, body, emotions, and spiritual healing requirements. By looking at all of these areas, you can distinguish patterns and habits that require positive change.

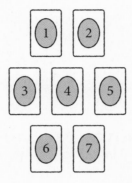

1. What does my body need more of?

2. What does my body need less of?

3. How can I support my mental health?

4. How can I support my emotional needs?

5. How can I support my spiritual healing?

6. What healing modality should I work with?

7. What healing buddy do I need?

Heal My Body Spell

I love nothing more when I'm sick than a hot cup of soup, and the spell for the Queen of Pentacles is a kitchen witch's healing potion disguised as vegan vegetable soup. You can add shredded chicken if you want some meat protein with your soup. Kitchen witches have long known that the herbs and spices put in broths and soups hold healing powers. This soup can also help boost your immune system if you're feeling like you're fighting off something. Adjust the vegetables if you don't like something that's been suggested. Soups are magic potions; don't discount them because they're everyday meals.

Best time to cast: Anytime

You will need

- Roasting tray
- One garlic bulb
- One onion
- One sweet potato
- Two bell peppers
- One carrot
- Olive or avocado oil
- Salt
- Pepper
- One and a half teaspoons of cum
- One and a half teaspoons of paprika
- Two sprigs of fresh rosemary
- Two sprigs of fresh thyme
- Pot
- Four cups of vegetable stock
- Hand blender

Cut your vegetables into chunks and place them on the roasting tray. Put a whole garlic bulb on the tray with the skin on. Sprinkle the vegetables with oil, salt, pepper, cumin, and paprika. Place in the oven, heated to 350°F. Just as the vegetables are getting soft, around thirty minutes, put a couple of sprigs of rosemary and thyme in the oven. If you place them in the oven with the vegetables in the beginning, they may burn. When the vegetables are soft and cooked through, add them to a pot, squeeze the garlic out of the skins into the pot, and take the leaves off the rosemary and thyme. Add four cups of vegetable stock and bring to a simmer. Then, slowly blend the soup with your blender—season to your personal taste.

King of Pentacles

Key concepts: Management, business acumen, maturity, support

This King is well and truly grounded; they know who they are and their strengths. They like having a good plan with clearly defined steps and outcomes. This is a welcome card when seeking answers in business and money readings.

Will This Business Succeed? Spread

The tarot spread for the King of Pentacles may save you from making a mistake on a business that'll go nowhere. You may be offered a management position with a company and want to ensure they're going to be around for the long haul. You may be looking at investing in a business or even starting one of your own.

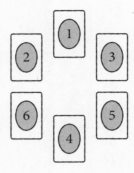

1. What is the current financial status of the business?
2. What impact will I have on the business?
3. Is this business a good fit for my skills?
4. What is the competition doing that this business needs to start doing?
5. How do I get a competitive edge?
6. What is the potential future of the business?

Boost Your Business Spell

Building a successful business doesn't stop even when you're in the black and reaching your goals. Markets change, technology changes, and getting people's attention is harder and harder. This spell can be cast when you feel like your business has hit a lull or is in danger of grinding to a halt. If you can't burn this incense blend, you can make it into a spray by using oils and water instead of herbs and spices.

Best time to cast: Anytime

You will need

- One High John the Conqueror root or powder
- One Lucky Hand root or powder
- Bergamot dried herb or essential oil
- Cinnamon chips or powder
- Incense-burning charcoal disks
- Lighter or matches
- Firesafe container or incense burner
- Mortar and pestle and/or coffee bean grinder

This is a business success incense blend. Combine all of the magical ingredients while chanting, "My business thrives, my business grows, I'm booked and blessed, everyone knows." You then want to burn this incense around your business or work space while you keep saying the chant. You can make more of this potent powder and do this whenever you need a business bump. Store your blend in an airtight glass container and keep it out of direct sunlight.

Magic Tip

While there is something very witchy about using a mortar and pestle to make your incense blends, some dried roots make it all but impossible to get a good mix. Having a small electric coffee bean blender to make tougher components into small pieces is really handy. Then, you can add those to your mortar and pestle and put your power into it while you finish making the blend.

Conclusion

I hope you've found seventy-eight new tarot spreads and spells you can work within your practice. I hope that you bookmark these pages and use the spreads in readings for yourself, your loved ones, and even clients. I hope you adapt a spell that resonates with you and lovingly hand-write it in your own Book of Shadows.

Tarot readings with magical spells are a fantastic way to expand your understanding of yourself and how the tarot can come to life. Like any tool, you need to use it to understand it fully. Experience is the greatest teacher. This book may be a jumping-off point for you to look at the tarot in a new way or try a spell for the first time.

Remember that it's your journey no matter where your magical road leads you. Embrace your successes and mistakes. Get your hands dirty by exploring new herbs and spices in your magical work. Try working with an elemental magic you've avoided or don't usually resonate with. Lean into those tarot cards that keep coming up for you or that you're afraid of. There are lessons, magic, and blessings in all of those places.

May you weave the magic of the tarot into your daily life as a way to understand yourself, your connection with your inner power, and the universe. May the seventy-eight cards be a loyal companion throughout your life as they have been for me.

Appendix 1
List of Tarot Spreads by Need

Love and Relationship Tarot Spreads

The Lovers—What Love Means to Me Spread

The Devil—Why Can't I Quit Them? Spread

Two of Cups—Where Is My True Love? Spread

Three of Cups—Friendship Spread

Seven of Cups—Is This Real? Spread

Knight of Cups—Hot Lover or a Dud? Spread

Queen of Wands—Is It All an Act? Spread

Knight of Swords—Mending a Fractured Relationship Spread

Home Tarot Spreads

The World—Potential New Home Spread

Ten of Cups—Happy Home Spread

Healing Tarot Spreads

The Empress—Healing the Mother Wound Spread

The Emperor—Healing the Father Wound Spread

The Hierophant—Healing the Institutional Wound Spread

Death—Mediumship Spread

Temperance—Healing Path Spread

Five of Cups—Feel to Heal Spread

Three of Swords—Listen to My Heartbreak Spread

Queen of Pentacles—How Can I Heal? Spread

Career and Work Tarot Spreads

Two of Wands—Is This Partnership a Good Idea? Spread

Three of Wands—Long-Term Goal Spread

Six of Wands—Be Victorious Spread

Ten of Wands—Delegate It, Stubborn Spread

Two of Pentacles—Work vs. Life Spread

Seven of Pentacles—Work Smarter Spread

King of Pentacles—Will This Business Succeed? Spread

Money and Prosperity Tarot Spreads

King of Wands—Will I Be a Successful Entrepreneur? Spread

Ace of Pentacles—Grow Your Abundance Spread

Four of Pentacles—Stop Money Leaks Spread

Nine of Pentacles—The Road to Financial Independence Spread

Ten of Pentacles—Financial Stability Spread

Protection Tarot Spreads

The Tower—Cope with Sudden Change Spread

Page of Cups—Empathic Powers Spread

Seven of Wands—What Needs Protecting? Spread

Six of Swords—Support in the Storm Spread

Justice and Karmic Tarot Spreads

Justice—You Get What You Give Spread

Judgement—Outcome of Legal Matters Spread

King of Swords—The Higher Lesson Spread

Spiritual Tarot Spreads

The High Priestess—Spiritual Development Spread

The Hermit—Message from My Spirit Guides Spread

Death—Mediumship Spread

The Star—Make It Happen Spread

The Moon—Dream Interpretation Spread

Five of Pentacles—Hope in the Darkness Spread

Personal Growth Tarot Spreads

The Sun—Inner Happiness Spread

Ace of Cups—Tap into Your Emotions Spread

Eight of Cups—Should I Stay or Should I Go? Spread

Nine of Cups—Self-Love Spread

Page of Cups—Empathic Powers Spread

Queen of Cups—Self-Compassion Spread

King of Cups—Shadow Work Spread

Ace of Wands—Find Your Passion Spread

Five of Wands—Take On This Challenge Spread

Eight of Wands—Bust through Blocks Spread

Nine of Wands—Why Am I So Exhausted? Spread

Page of Wands—Playful Soul Spread

Knight of Wands—Find My Soul's Passion Spread

Four of Swords—Inner Peace Spread

Eight of Swords—Free Yourself Spread

Ten of Swords—How Can I Let It Go? Spread

Queen of Swords—Judge Judy Spread

Three of Pentacles—Long-Term Plans Spread

Six of Pentacles—Build Your Self-Worth Spread

Miscellaneous Tarot Spreads

The Fool—Take the Leap Spread

The Chariot—Torn Between Two Decisions Spread

Strength—Force Spread

Wheel of Fortune—Get Lucky Spread

The Hanged Man—Get Out of Limbo Spread

Four of Cups—Release Apathy Spread

Six of Cups—Past Life Spread

Four of Wands—Birthday Spread

Ace of Swords—Find Inspiration Spread

Two of Swords—Get Unstuck Spread

Five of Swords—Stop the Arguments Spread

Seven of Swords—Who's a Snake? Spread

Nine of Swords—Am I Cursed? Spread

Page of Swords—What's Really Going On? Spread

Eight of Pentacles—Is This Course Worth It? Spread

Page of Pentacles—Keep It Simple Spread

Knight of Pentacles—Am I Being Stubborn or Determined? Spread

Appendix 2
List of Spells by Need

Love and Relationship Spells

The Lovers—Come and Light My Fire Spell

Two of Cups—Call In My True Love Spell

Three of Cups—Find a New BFF Spell

Knight of Cups—Call In a New Lover Spell

Four of Wands—Newlywed Blessing

Home Spells

The World—New House Blessing

Ten of Cups—Home Harmony Spell Jar

Eight of Wands—Smooth Move Spell

Ten of Pentacles—Find the Perfect Home Spell

Healing Spells

The Empress—Fertility Spell

Temperance—Chakra Alignment and Healing Spell

The Sun—Heal Your Inner Child Spell

Three of Swords—Heal My Heart Spell

Page of Pentacles—Heal a Sick Animal Spell

Queen of Pentacles—Heal My Body Spell

Career and Work Spells

Two of Wands—Find the Perfect Work Partner Spell

King of Wands—Step into Leadership Spell

Knight of Swords—Manifest My Ideas Spell

Two of Pentacles—Stop Saying Yes at Work Spell

Three of Pentacles—Work Together Well Spell

Eight of Pentacles—Get Your Promotion Spell

Nine of Pentacles—More Clients and Customers Spell

King of Pentacles—Boost Your Business Spell

Money and Prosperity Spells

Ace of Pentacles—Unlimited Prosperity Spell

Four of Pentacles—Get My Money Back Spell

Five of Pentacles—Be Debt Free Spell

Protection Spells

The Chariot—Car Protection Spell

Strength—Protect My Child Spell

The Tower—Shock Absorption Talisman

Five of Cups—Safe Place to Grieve Spell

Page of Cups–Empath Protection Aura Spray
Seven of Wands–Mirror Protection Spell
Five of Swords–F-Off Energy Vampire Spell
Six of Swords–Travel Protection Spell
Nine of Swords–Banish Night Terrors Spell
Ten of Swords–Negative Vibes Removal Incense
Knight of Pentacles–Protect My Energy Necklace

Justice and Karmic Spells

Justice–Swift Justice Spell
Queen of Swords–Fairness Spell

Spiritual Spells

The Hierophant–Spiritual Guidance Spell

Personal Growth Spells

The Magician–Empowerment Tea Spell
The High Priestess–Psychic Powers Anointing Oil
Wheel of Fortune–Good Luck Spell
The Moon–Dream Recall Spell
Judgement–Stop Caring What Other People Think Spell
Ace of Cups–Tea of Peace Spell
Six of Cups–Release Past Chains Spell
Eight of Cups–Let It Go Spell
King of Cups–Shadow Integration Incense Blend
Ace of Wands–Ignite Your Inner Spark Spell
Three of Wands–Reach My Goals Spell
Six of Wands–Victory Spell

Knight of Wands–Winner Winner Spell

Queen of Wands–Reclaim Your Power Spell

Two of Swords–Clarity Spell

Eight of Swords–Cord Cutting Spell

Ten of Swords–Negative Vibes Removal Incense

King of Swords–First Choice College Spell

Miscellaneous Spells

The Fool–Have Faith Charm

The Emperor–Strong Constitution Spell

The Hermit–Wax Scrying Spell

The Hanged Man–Bring Change Now Spell

The Devil–Resist Temptation Spell

The Star–Make a Wish Spell

Four of Cups–Reengage Joy Spell

Seven of Cups–Sweet Fantasy Bath Spell

Nine of Cups–Love and Accept Me Spell

Queen of Cups–Third Eye Psychic Balm

Five of Wands–Have Courage Bracelet Spell

Nine of Wands–Energy Recovery Elixir

Ten of Wands–Let Go of Control Spell

Page of Wands–Wonder Spell

Ace of Swords–Bust through Writer's Block Spell

Four of Swords–Peaceful Sleep Oil

Seven of Swords–Gossip Stopping Spell

Six of Pentacles–Reach a Donation Goal Spell

Seven of Pentacles–Bountiful Harvest Spell

Recommended Resources

These are books and resources for readers to explore in order to expand their tarot practice. I've provided a brief description of the resources and why I recommend them.

Tarot Readers Academy

I established the Tarot Readers Academy was established in 2015 as a place for tarot students and enthusiasts to learn about the art of tarot readings, divination, and magic. There are programs available for all levels of tarot readers, including free tutorials and resources, which can all be found at tarotreadersacademy.com.

Modern Witchcraft and Wicca Books

This list of books includes essential books that I recommend to students who want to learn about modern Wicca and Witchcraft. They'll give you a solid place to start forming your own path if you wish to work as a solitary practitioner or find a coven.

When, Why…If: An Ethics Workbook—Robin Wood. This book is essential for practitioners who want to understand their biases and the morals and ethics of practicing witchcraft.

The Witch's Shield—Christopher Penczak. A great book full of information and practical exercises to protect yourself in and outside of the magical circle. Penzack will lead you from beginner techniques of protection work to more advanced energetic magic, so you have a well-developed practice at the end of the book.

Wheels of Life: A User's Guide to the Chakra System—Anodea Judith. A thorough exploration of the chakras and how they come into play in your spiritual practice. It will give you a foundation for working with the chakra system with additional complimentary esoteric knowledge.

Psychic Witch—Mat Auryn. This book is a must-read for learning how to develop your energetic practice. This includes meditation, tuning in, the astral realms, and more. There are exercises for the beginner, where you'll be walked through each step to ensure you'll be successful. It is valuable to anyone who wants to develop their connection to their psychic abilities.

Wicca and *Living Wicca*—Scott Cunningham. These two are classic Wicca books that are on the recommended reading list for many working covens and teaching circles. These books will give you a solid foundation so you can forge your own path.

The Craft—Dorothy Morrison. This modern witches' Book of Shadows will teach you many things about witchcraft and inspire you to work with your own magical books.

Rebel Witch—Kelly-Ann Maddox. A modern and deeply magical approach to witchcraft. Kelly-Ann encourages the reader to find their own practice and connection to the Divine and themselves. It's personal, engaging, and full of modern witchcraft practices.

Magical Correspondence and Spell Books

Every modern mystic needs reference books for their work. These books will help you write your own spells. Learn more about magical ingredients that will be used in your practice for years.

Cunningham's Encyclopedia of Crystal, Gem & Metal Magic—Scott Cunningham. This book covers the magical energies of crystals and gems. It's easy to use and find what you're looking for, making it a volume to keep at arm's length when writing your own spells.

The Master Book of Herbalism—Paul Beyerl. This book is one I always recommend when it comes to herbs and their magical energies. If there is one book on magical herbs you're going to get, make it this one. It has traditional, medicinal, and magical correspondences for essential herbs and spices for the magic practitioner to reference throughout their journey.

The Complete Book of Incense, Oils and Brews—Scott Cunningham. Another solid and invaluable book by Cunningham. This book will aid you in developing your work with magical blends of all kinds for your rituals and spells.

Llewellyn's Complete Book of Correspondences—Sandra Kynes. This massive reference book will quickly become full of your own notes and stick tabs for when you're making magic. The format makes it easy to use and understand.

The Book of Candle Magic—Madame Pamita. This is excellent for those who want to work with candle magic and its many applications in spells. It's perfect for the beginner candle magic practitioner. There are potent spells from Madame Pamita and instructions to create your own.

The Element Encyclopedia of 5000 Spells—Judika Illes. From simple spells to more extended rituals, there is a spell for pretty much everything in this book. You can use the works here verbatim, or you can use them as inspiration for you to write your own spells for your specific needs.

Tarot Books

A robust tarot book library is a must for those looking to have a well-rounded tarot practice. These are books that I recommend for students and seasoned tarot readers. These books are a great place to continue your tarot education and inspiration. Many of the authors on this list have a number of books available, and they're wonderful.

Holistic Tarot—Benebell Wen. This book is a deep well of knowledge that will allow you to add different layers to your readings and learn about yourself along the way. In this book, you can use the tarot cards for more than divination readings. You'll learn how to use the tarot to make decisions, gain clarity, and be more mindful in your life.

78 Degrees of Wisdom—Rachel Pollack. This book is a classic and a must-read for all tarot readers. Without this vital book, tarot wouldn't be where it is today. Rachel takes you on a journey through each of the cards, weaving philosophy, esotericism, and divination with each tarot card.

Tarot for Your Self—Mary K. Greer. Another classic that all tarot students and readers must read. It's not only a fantastic tarot read, but it's also a book that will allow you to learn about yourself in a profound way. If you want to find a personal connection with the tarot, this is the book to start with.

The Tarot Coloring Book—Theresa Reed. This book is a great way to discover each card. By coloring each of the cards, you'll find all of the symbols within and form a bond with the cards. Theresa also includes solid information about the tarot throughout the book, making learning the tarot fun and creative.

Advanced Tarot—Paul Fenton-Smith. Paul has been reading the tarot and teaching for decades. His book will keep you engaged, as it's chocked full of wisdom. This book gives you the ability to see the tarot in a variety of ways in each reading. Beginner tarot readers and advanced readers will get a lot out of this book.

The Ultimate Guide to Tarot—Liz Dean. A volume full of information on each tarot card and classic tarot spreads from a well-respected tarot author and teacher. It's well organized, allowing you to get the information you need quickly. It's also full of tips and techniques you can use in your readings immediately.

The Magic of Tarot—Sasha Graham. A magical book of ritual and practice for any tarot reader who wants to do more with their readings. This book is easy to understand, making the information and exercises easy to incorporate into your personal practice.

Tarot Deciphered—T. Susan Chang, M. M. Meleen. This book is going to take you on a journey with each card. You'll learn about the mythology, alchemy, and other esoteric elements that come into play with the tarot. It's a valuable resource to bring depth into your readings and to decipher common symbols you may get stuck on.

The Big Book of Tarot—Joan Bunnings. Joan's first book is iconic, and her website was one of the first robust and credible tarot resources on the internet. *The Big Book of Tarot* is her classic's new, expanded edition. There's now even more to enjoy with this cornerstone tarot book, whether you use the book in its lesson format or look up individual tarot card meanings.

Bibliography

Bennett, Robin. *Healing Magic: A Green Witch Guidebook to Conscious Living, 10th Anniversary Edition.* Berkeley, CA: North Atlantic Books, 2014.

Beyerl, Paul. *The Master Book of Herbalism.* Blaine, WA: Phoenix Publishing, 1984.

Bunnings, Joan. *The Big Book of Tarot: How to Interpret the Cards and Work with Tarot Spreads for Personal Growth.* Newburyport, MA: Weiser Books, 2019.

Chang, T. Susan. *Tarot Correspondences: Ancient Secrets for Everyday Readers.* Woodbury, MN: Llewellyn Publications, 2018.

Conway, D. J. *Moon Magick: Myth & Magic, Crafts & Recipes, Rituals & Spells.* Woodbury, MN: Llewellyn Publications, 2014.

Cunningham, Scott. *Cunningham's Encyclopedia of Crystal, Gem & Metal Magic.* Woodbury, MN: Llewellyn Publications, 2002.

Cunningham, Scott. *The Complete Book of Incense, Oils and Brews*. Woodbury, MN: Llewellyn Publications, 2009.

Hall, Judy. *The Crystal Bible*. Iola, WI: Krause Publications, 2003.

Judith, Anodea. *Wheels of Life: A User's Guide to the Chakra System*. Woodbury, MN: Llewellyn Publications, 2012.

Katz, Michael. *Gemstone Energy Medicine: Healing Body, Mind and Spirit*. Rochester, VT: Natural Healing Press, 2013.

King, Scott Alexander. *World Animal Dreaming: Interpreting the Symbolic Language of the World's Animals*. Queensland, Australia: Animal Dreaming Publication, 2023.

Kynes, Sandra. *Llewellyn's Complete Book of Correspondences: A Comprehensive & Cross-Referenced Resource for Pagans & Wicans*. Woodbury, MN: Llewellyn Publications, 2013.

Melody. *Love Is in the Earth: A Kaleidoscope of Crystals*. Wheat Ridge, CO: Earth-Love Pub House, 1995.

Nozedar, Adele. *The Illustrated Signs & Symbols Sourcebook*. New York: Harper, 2010.

Parker, Julia, and Derek Parker. *Parkers' Astrology: The Definitive Guide to Using Astrology in Every Aspect of Your Life*. London: Penguin Books, 2001.

Place, Robert. *The Tarot: History, Symbolism, and Divination*. New York: TarcherPerigee, 2005.

Raven, Gwion. *The Magick of Food: Rituals, Offerings & Why We Eat Together*. Woodbury, MN: Llewellyn Publications, 2020.

Tahoma, Koko. *Native American Herbalist's Bible: The Most Complete Step-By-Step Herbal Dispensatory*.Self-published, 2023.

Telesco, Patricia. *Shaman in a 9 to 5 World*. Berkeley, CA: Ten-Speed Press, 2000.

Thomson, Sandra A. *Pictures from the Heart: A Tarot Dictionary*. New York: St. Martin's Griffin, 2003.

Wen, Benebell. *Holistic Tarot*. Berkeley, CA: North Atlantic Books, 2015.

Wilde, Oscar. *Lady Windermere's Fan*. New York: Samuel French, 1893.

To Write to the Author

If you wish to contact the author or would like more information about this book, please write to the author in care of Llewellyn Worldwide Ltd. and we will forward your request. Both the author and the publisher appreciate hearing from you and learning of your enjoyment of this book and how it has helped you. Llewellyn Worldwide Ltd. cannot guarantee that every letter written to the author can be answered, but all will be forwarded. Please write to:

Ethony Dawn
℅ Llewellyn Worldwide
2143 Wooddale Drive
Woodbury, MN 55125-2989

Please enclose a self-addressed stamped envelope for reply,
or $1.00 to cover costs. If outside the U.S.A., enclose
an international postal reply coupon.

Many of Llewellyn's authors have websites with additional information and resources. For more information, please visit our website at http://www.llewellyn.com.